BEFORE OUR TIME:

An Oral History of St. John

Janet Burton

Printed in the United States of America

ISBN: 978-0-9906441-0-1

Cover Photo by Tony Scimeca

Naomi Jacobs with her hoop baskets and wist products, including coasters, mats, and sandwich trays. The broom is made from tyre palm.

Emmaus Moravian Church in the background.

www.oralhistoryofstjohn.com

DEDICATION

To my grandmother, Helen Smith Prince.

To my mother, Naomi Prince Jacobs.

To my son, Jonathan Joseph Burton, who read and owned hundreds of books as a child because reading is important.

Contents

Preface

As a very young child I sat in the lap of my grandmother, Helen Prince, who read books to me while she sat in her rocking chair. It is my earliest memory, because I was too young to attend school at the time. As she read and we rocked, it was such a pleasurable experience that not only did I gain immediate satisfaction, but that simple activity was instrumental in determining my goals and the career path I would take in life.

Books were not easy to come by. There were no libraries or bookstores anywhere on the island of St. John. So, after I learned to read, I just read what was available. One book that we had was the Walter Field Catalog. Most likely there were few homes at that time that didn't have one, because many families either had a seamstress make their clothing or they ordered items from Walter Field and paid when the package arrived. I read the Walter Field Catalog from front to back.

Sometimes when I was reading I would lie on my bed or on our sofa that my grandmother and great uncle slept on as children. Of course, these would be times when everybody else was outside working. I was also supposed to be doing my chores. When I heard my mother, Naomi, coming I would throw the book behind the sofa or under the bed. She never acted like she heard anything. But when we spoke as adults once, she said, "You think I didn't know what you were doing?" It made me appreciate her more to find out that she indulged me and did not stop me from reading and learning in order to do household chores.

While I was a student at Benjamin Franklin School in Coral Bay, the Coxes settled there. Mrs. Cox had hundreds of books and created the first library in Coral Bay in the Fellowship Hall of Emmaus Moravian Church. It was open on Saturdays so that was where I would be each Saturday until I completed the eighth grade.

When I moved to St. Thomas to attend the Charlotte Amalie High School I had to have a guardian because it was impossible to commute on a daily basis. I lived with Mrs. Elsa Hughes who thought I shouldn't do housework because I was a paying guest ($20/month for room and board). I was thirteen years old and secretly agreed with her. So each afternoon after I got home from school and put my books down, I would head out the door to my new-found love, the Enid Baa Public Library.

I would check out two books, usually mysteries, go home, have dinner, and read until I finished. The next day I would do the same thing again. I hardly did homework, because we had none at Benjamin Franklin School. There, our notebooks with material copied from the board stayed in our desks and we played marbles all the way home.

Long story short. I became a teacher and subsequently a librarian. Along the way, in the 1970's I became fascinated by oral history. Although it appealed to me, it was after I returned home as a librarian, first at Charlotte Amalie High School and then at Julius Sprauve School in St. John, that it piqued my interest again.

We used Ruth Moolenaar's, *Profiles of Outstanding Virgin Islanders,* quite extensively during Black History Month when students were assigned reports on local persons of achievement. One day when I saw Mrs.

Moolenaar, I said to her: "Why haven't you included more St. Johnians in your books?" She challenged me by saying, "Why don't you write about them?" Her words were the stimulus that got me started.

I envisioned a publication that would combine biographical material with oral history and illustration which would be appealing to youngsters from middle school to adults. The children are the main reason that this labor of love began. I write for all the students I taught and the ones I don't know and will never know. I want them to know what St. John was like for persons like my mother who was born almost 100 years ago in 1921 and for her contemporaries. I want them to get to know people like her, who may not have a structure or space named in their honor, but who were instrumental in passing on the culture and history of this special place, St. John, U.S. Virgin Islands. She motivated me to love and preserve our story.

Some persons I interviewed were eager to share their family history. Thecla Jurgen Hanley and Louisa Stevens Duzant were so animated about their fathers, that I didn't have to ask any questions. They just ran with the topic and gave all the information while I took a back seat; so, I have given them the credit for their accounts.

Others were more reluctant to part with their stories. I made appointments with one gentleman several times but he never gave any information about his father who was a fascinating subject.

The most interesting part of my work was the interviews. I did not always guide, but let them take on a life of their own. This allowed me to capture information I might have otherwise missed had I stuck to a rigid format of questions. Above all, my goal has been for the reader to hear the voice of the interviewee.

Opportunities to learn about the interview process and other aspects of oral history presented themselves. I attended a comprehensive Oral History Workshop coordinated by the Virgin Islands Humanities Council, on December 8–9, 1989 in St. Thomas and another in St. John on April 3, 1995 presented by Dr. Karen Olwig under the auspices of the St. John Oral History Association.

While the interviews were underway, assistance was provided by the St. John Ancestral Preservation Committee. One of the members of the Association, Miss Nancy Gotwalt, served as treasurer, bought secretarial supplies, and dispensed a small stipend for incidental expenses.

Introduction

Internationally, the 1940's was a time when World War II ended and the United Nations was formed. Nationally, RCA introduced 45 rpm records, and Jackie Robinson became the first African American baseball player. In St. Thomas, U.S. Virgin Islands, the price of gasoline increased to 28 cents per gallon and three men were fined $5, $4, and $3 for using obscene language on the street.

On St. John, Austin Walters operated the first electric power plant; Julius E. Sprauve, Sr. represented St. John as a Member of the Municipal Council; Guy Benjamin was an educator; Leander Jurgen and Joshua Stevens had just begun their careers as policemen; Elaine Sprauve worked in the office of the St. John Administrator; Ella Samuel Hodge was a church organist; and Naomi Prince Jacobs, an accomplished craftsperson, gave birth to the author of this book.

I interviewed Mr. Austin Walters on January 9, 1992. At one time I had planned to write a book about him. As a child, I knew that he and my uncle Austin Smith were the first two people to drive from Cruz Bay to Coral Bay. That seemed worthy of documentation because the road at that time was not paved.

Mr. Walters was eager to tell his story. He is the only person in the book who is not a St. Johnian. As you read about him, you will see why he is chosen.

He immersed himself in day to day life in St. John and was very innovative, applying all the various skills and knowledge he used in St. Thomas to improve government and move St. John forward.

My cousin, Guy Benjamin, wrote about himself in his books. Various magazine articles were written about him. Because of his influence on education in St. John, he had to be included.

Mr. Sprauve fought tenaciously to improve conditions in St. John. One of his battles was for good roads, especially one that could take vehicular traffic between Cruz Bay and Coral Bay. Another was for homestead-ing. Many individuals were able to purchase property at an affordable cost to erect residences.

Ella Samuel Hodge was a musician and entrepreneur who had many talents. She began to work at an early age and didn't stop until she couldn't go any more. One of her outside jobs was as a clerk in Mr. Sprauve's grocery store in Cruz Bay.

Captain Leander Jurgen and Patrolman Joshua Stevens were responsible for keeping the peace on the island. Capt. Jurgen covered Cruz Bay and Patrolman Stevens was in charge of Coral Bay. Other officers were added to the force as time went on.

A gracious and intelligent lady, Elaine Sprauve, kept the government running efficiently at its headquarters in the Battery. We always assumed she knew everything there was to know to keep the office functioning properly. She was not the Administrator, because she didn't wish to be. She was Mr. Sprauve's sister-in-law, so besides being in a position of power in the Executive Department, she was closely connected to the representative of the Legislative Department.

My mother, Naomi Prince Jacobs, graces the cover of the book along with some of the articles she made with native vines — hoop and wist. She made me drive all over St. John to pick maran bush to wash dishes, because that was what her mother used. She treasured the past, but was totally in the present and loved controversial topics like religion and politics. The family thought she might have been a good lawyer if she'd had the opportunity to further her education. Like Mrs. Ella, she worked in one of Mr. Sprauve's grocery stores — the shop in Palestina, Coral Bay.

Regarding the format, I have tried to keep the students in mind by breaking up the material into segments, much like a chapter book. This way they can flip through and see if something jumps out at them and stop to read it. Perhaps then, they will be snared and will want to go to the beginning and read the entire piece.

For place names, I have used the spellings in the Department of Commerce's *Geographic Dictionary of the Virgin Islands of the United States* by James William McGuire, Washington, Government Printing Office, 1925.

Acknowledgments

I am thankful to Mr. Elroy Sprauve, Mrs. Thecla Jurgen Hanley, Mrs. Louisa Stevens Duzant and her sister, Mathilda Stevens Harvey and Mrs. Jean Nicholson Gibbs, for material and interviews; to Dr. Gilbert Sprauve, Mr. Elroy Sprauve, Mrs. Mary Dorn, Miss Nancy Gotwalt and Mrs. Pamela Richards Samuel for reading the interviews and giving constructive advice; to Dan and Mary Jo Schmiesing of St. Henry, Ohio, for the photograph of their Red Poll cows; to photographers: Mrs. Cristina Kessler, Mr. Oriel Smith, Mr. Oswin Sewer, Sr., and Mr. Warren Wells, Jr.; to other persons who provided photographs: Mr. Elroy Sprauve, Mrs. Yvonne Wells, Mrs. Thecla Jurgen Hanley; and to Mrs. Lee Stanciauskas for her invaluable assistance in getting the manuscript ready to print; as well as family, friends and well-wishers like Miss Nancy Gotwalt, Mr. Leayle "Manny" Pickering, Jr., Mr. Spencer Archibald, Mr. Evan Williams and many others to whom I am indebted for moral support and encouragement during the journey.

Guy Henry Benjamin
October 18, 1913 – June 19, 2012

Guy Benjamin

GUY BENJAMIN was passionate about learning, writing, music and dominoes. He loved people, animals and St. John.

Mr. Benjamin was born on October 18, 1913 in East End, St. John, Danish West Indies to Cassilda Henry January and Harold Benjamin. He lived in Palestina and moved to East End as a child where he had a happy childhood before going to St. Thomas to live with the Amos Benjamin, Sr. family, his cousins, who had known him previously due to their East End visits. He became the first St. Johnian to graduate from high school in St. Thomas in 1934. He and another classmate attended their 75th Reunion in 2009.

Most likely, Mr. Benjamin was also the first St. Johnian to take advantage of higher education in Puerto Rico. He stated:

"I attended the University of Puerto Rico on a scholarship from the Department of Education for the summer—6 weeks. I loved the bell tower, beautiful girls, learned to love Puerto Rican food. I lived with a family within walking distance of the University.

I studied English, Art and Spanish. Some classes were in Spanish: The New School and Teaching. I observed classes in math. I enjoyed the movies and a Casals Concert given by the University. My credits were all accepted by Howard University. I had enough to be a sophomore.

Howard University was a change from the University of Puerto Rico. Instead of having classes in Spanish and English, I had them in English alone. I lived in a YMCA until I could share an apartment with another student who was majoring in law. We both worked and went to school. His classes were during the day and mine at night. Sometimes I didn't see him for a whole week, until weekends. Now he's a judge in Virginia and we still correspond.

At Howard, I majored in English and the Classics. It was a new experience. I found out the teachers there were so dedicated to their students—one would invite all her "foreign" students to her home for Thanksgiving dinner.

She made them feel at home and wanted.

One summer I did three Humanities—Humanities I, II, and III—three reading courses. I found that the high schools in St. Thomas were on a par with other high schools in the U.S. As an undergraduate, I substituted as an English teacher there when there was a need.

Another experience at Howard was when I sent home to get my high school algebra and geometry grades. The records couldn't be found. I was advised to check the archives in D.C. So I had to take algebra and geometry during my senior year at Howard. I had enough credits in psychology and my teacher advised that after the first day I teach the class. So I taught the class under his supervision.

I found friends at Howard who accepted me as a brother and I cannot forget my experiences there. I met many African students. They invited me home to Nigeria, saying there was land I could have. I had to work, so I couldn't find time to attend their fraternity.

While I was at Howard there was no Moravian Church, so I attended Methodist, sang with the choir, and substituted as pianist for the Sunday School class.

I had a club for the children where they could come to my house and have parties on Saturday nights but their parents had to come too.

Howard had the prettiest girls of all the nationalities you could name. Many Jewish students were admitted to medical school there."

After receiving his Bachelor's degree at Howard University, Benji continued on studying English and the Classics at New York University, where he got his Master's degree.

"At New York University, it was study, cram, study. When you work days and go to school at night you never have time for much, but I did get in opera, ballet and plays at student rates even if it was only standing room. I did graduate studies there. I did administration [classes] from NYU here.

The origin of classes was the hardest course I had at NYU. Two of 32 students passed it and I was one.

One of the good things about NYU and their part in upgrading teachers in the VI was their ability to bring in the best teachers to lead us in administration and education classes.

During my NYU days, supervisors and administrators in the Department of Education had the advantage of going to the best school in the U.S. for six weeks in the summer. We took part in training teachers for the Peace Corps.

The best offer I had was to transfer from the USVI as Superintendent of Education to the University of San Francisco and continue as a preparing teacher for teachers going overseas. It fell through when San Francisco lost their Federal Government contract. So I trained at Columbia University to go to the Peace Corps. I got sick and didn't make it to Africa after all. Of the 140 [persons] training at Columbia I was picked as one of the ones most likely to succeed.

I took courses towards a Ph.D. and went to Chattanooga, N.Y. and sang on the same program with the Mormon Tabernacle Choir of about 200 voices."

Guy Benjamin School, formerly known as Benjamin Franklin School

Photo: Janet Burton

Mr. Benjamin came home and brought his beloved aunts from East End—Inger and Miriam (Mirrie)— to live with him. They never knew from one minute to the next if he was going to send a hungry child home from Benjamin Franklin School for them to feed one of their "emergency lunches" or if he himself was going to dash in the house to get a t-shirt for a student whose clothes he had to wash.

Guy Benjamin taught at Abraham Lincoln (later J. Antonio Jarvis School, now closed), and Thomas Jefferson School (Jarvis Annex, also closed) in St. Thomas. In St John, he was a teacher at Horace Mann School (closed as well) in Johns Folly; the Bethany School (which preceded the Julius E. Sprauve School) in Cruz Bay; and in Coral Bay he served as Principal/Teacher at Benjamin Franklin School, whose name was changed to his by Legislative Act 3695, recognizing his more than 40 years of devoted and distinguished service in the Virgin Islands Department of Education. Unfortunately that school also closed in June 2014.

He moved up the ranks from classroom teacher to Principal of the Benjamin Franklin School, Education Officer for St. John, Coordinator of Educational Programs on St. John, and District Superintendent of Schools, St. Thomas/St. John. He retired in 1974. That same year, Resolution 714 was approved by the Virgin Islands Legislature to honor and congratulate him for over forty years of "distinguished and faithful service to the people of the Virgin Islands as an outstanding leader and educator in the Virgin Islands Department of Education."

Mr. Benjamin's classes were always interesting and challenging. He would bring his records from home and have music appreciation sessions. His pupils had time to get lost in volumes of The Book of Knowledge and find out all sorts of wonderful things. There were spelling bees and excursions, mini-field trips like going down to the dock and sitting by the sea, to hear him read Huckleberry Finn. He loved to learn his entire life always reading, writing, and traveling. He inspired and empowered many by teaching and example.

Something that was very gratifying to him was to see children on the boats and buses going to school in St. Thomas and being aware he played a role in their transportation. His second greatest satisfaction was seeing his students produce the way they are doing. He felt his time wasn't wasted and knowing what he was doing will still be carried on is something else he admired.

He said:

Gregre tree foliage
(bucida buceras)

Photo: Forest & Kim Starr

"I started by finding a place that could take 7 or 8 students who graduated from 8th grade (the highest grade on the island at that time) to stay in St. Thomas with Mrs. Nicholson, who was the most appropriate person.

The next thing was transportation by bus, boat, and car when boats ran daily—so many connections had to be made from John's Folly (farthest point south of Coral Bay where students lived).

One night it rained for hours. The students from St. John couldn't stay at Charlotte Amalie High School and I wanted them to come home. I went to Cruz Bay in the rain and got Mr. Sullivan to go for them by boat. The boat almost turned around and we turned back to St. Thomas. The guts came down and we had to go over the hill. Finally, we got to the high school. The kids were there. We brought them home and not long after they went to sleep they had to get up and go back to school.

We started transporting students by Rodney's (Rodney Varlack) boat to St. Thomas and using his buses to transport students within St. John. Kendell Anthony

Gregre tree (bucida buceras)

Photo: Forest & Kim Starr

Guy Benjamin seated at church organ.

Coal pot in which fire was created with charcoal, small sticks and a match or live coal. Two old door hinges would be placed on top, upon which the pot of food sat until cooked.

Photo: Janet Burton

brought the students from East End to Coral Bay, first by boat and then later by vehicle. Mrs. Anna Sewer transported the ones from John's Folly.

As Education Officer, I got flush toilets and showers installed at Benjamin Franklin and Julius Sprauve schools, and a more automatic thing at Horace Mann. At Sprauve School it required digging up the street and running the lines to the Creek. This was accomplished by the Department of Education and the Public Works Department with support from the community.

I started the School lunch program in St. John. Kids coming from Mary's Point, Coral Bay, Bordeaux, daily without lunch broke my heart because they would spend recess playing, snatch up some water and go all day. I took the problem to Mr. Dixon and discussed it with him. He said he would keep it in mind. One day he called and said if we could get some food and utensils how can we manage without a kitchen. I said if they could get food and utensils, no problem. I would store it and the parents and students would help us. So whatever he got for Benjamin Franklin he got for Sprauve and Horace Mann. This was before the roads were paved so he made arrangements for boats to go to Cruz Bay with food, then come to Coral Bay and stop off at Friis for John's Folly's food.

The students would cook under the "gregre tree" (at Benjamin Franklin) then parents would come and help when possible. We cooked with three stones and wood and then about 2 coal pots came from St. Thomas. Boys would pick wood on their way to school and drop off a little bundle. The top student in cooking [Charlotte Harley] when she left here applied for a school lunch position in New York and became the head school lunch worker at her school there.

Mr. Theovald [Moorehead] became Senator and we started to move by leaps and bounds. We got flush toilets then and showers. Thanks to Dixon, Roebuck (maintenance man from St. Thomas) and Moorehead.

As Education Officer, I also departmentalized Sprauve School. I worked closely with Sprauve and when I got something for Benjamin Franklin School, I got it for Sprauve School also.

A car was assigned to me and I had to use it for going to Sprauve, Horace Mann and East End Schools. Dr. Arthur Richards was Commissioner of Education and took money from St. Croix's budget and bought a car for St. John. Itinerant teachers were transported [from Cruz Bay] by that car to work at Benjamin Franklin School.

Teachers were taking courses from New York

University. All Principals went once a week for classes in Administration and curriculum building. Different professors would come from NYU. Credits were earned. St. John Principals had to go to St. Thomas and Mr. [Herman] Prince (basketry teacher) would take over Horace Mann when Mr. Dunn [Principal] left. Classes were on Friday."

East End, in his youth, was a community in which there were excellent singers and musicians. Mr. Benjamin was exposed to that. However, it was his lifelong friend Ella Samuel Hodge, two and a half years older, who taught him to play the piano. When he moved to St. Thomas, he lived with a family who loved and were involved in music too.

Donkeys

Photo: Cristina Kessler

He played the organ at Emmaus Church whenever he could. About 60 years ago he had a youth choir, mostly girls whom he trained to sing soprano and alto. His most famous choir was the Guy Benjamin Chorale which sang during the 1970's and '80's. They sang at different churches in St. John and appeared on television in St. Thomas. Members of the all male a capella group ranged from students at Benjamin Franklin School to adults. He, himself, sang a most beautiful bass and was a member of the choir at Emmaus until six months before he died at 98.

Besides Emmaus, Mr. Benjamin filled in as organist for the Catholic and Anglican Churches in Cruz Bay and for his Sunday School class in Washington, D.C. while he was a student at Howard University.

An attempt was made to start a church choir when Benji must have been in his late 80's or so. He practiced and practiced the group who was coming to come (getting there, improving), but never got good enough (in his opinion) to sing before the congregation and so they never did. He demanded excellence in performance and would not settle for mediocrity.

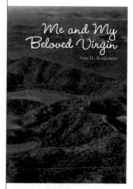

Me and My Beloved Virgin (1998)

Benji always had an organ or piano or both in his home in St. John as well as in his apartment in New York where he lived half of the year after retirement for many years before relocating to Coral Bay.

Mr. Benjamin was a domino fiend. He would go

to Fred's in Cruz Bay, to relatives' homes, wherever, to play his favorite game. He played to win and win he did a great deal of the time. Less than a week before he died, he played competitively, winning one or two games.

Benji loved family. Once he did extensive research on his family tree that culminated in a huge chart. He helped raise some of his relatives and had a wide circle of friends of different nationalities and races. He opened his heart, his house, and his wallet to many, very many.

In his yard, donkeys, birds and resident fowls (geese, ducks, etc.) dined. His place was their Coral Bay stomping ground. The donkeys had a schedule and came in different shifts. Years ago one of them got inside the house which was never locked. He took bread from the refrigerator for himself and knocked down some eggs for the dog. It might have been that same dog and a goat who spent the night in bed with Benjy during a hurricane, one at his head, one at his feet. When the winds got severe, the dog howled and the goat bleated – each, in turn, lamenting the terrible situation, receiving consolation no doubt from their human friend.

This gentleman who was St. John's Renaissance Man wrote two books: *Me and My Beloved Virgin*, published in 1981 and *More Tales of Me and My Beloved Virgin* which came out in 1983. For some years they have been combined in one volume. Through his remarkable voice we can all experience a past, primarily St. Johnian, that few can still remember. We can all be grateful to him for its preservation. Besides his major works, he did extensive research on the community of East End as well as other writings.

Among Mr. Benjamin's many talents were teaching, writing, singing, playing piano and organ, cooking, and master domino player. He had the first cinema in Coral Bay in the old wooden multipurpose building (police station, clinic and kindergarten classroom) located on the grounds of the Benjamin Franklin School later known as Guy Benjamin School.

"Benji", as he was affectionately called, was a man who achieved much and gained recognition locally and abroad, but was humble and a total people person. He would have given away all his money to friends looking for a handout without thinking twice. He always found time to talk to family and friends, whether in person or on the telephone. Once when a relative was seriously ill in the hospital in St. Thomas, he sent a get-well card every day for over a month from New York. Although his achievements were impressive, what is woven throughout the fabric of his life is a singular commitment to education in St. John.

Some of his students remember him as a disciplinarian. It does take some degree of discipline to teach four grades at a time. At the Benjamin Franklin School, he taught grades 5, 6, 7, and 8 in the same classroom all day. There were no special teachers, like gym or Spanish in those days, to give classroom teachers a planning period. But, strict as he might be, he was also a compassionate person who took care of the students as if they were his own children.

Ella Jane Samuel Hodge
May 29, 1911 – January 19, 2012

ELLA SAMUEL HODGE, whose youthful ambition was to become a nurse so she could see inside people, instead became a music teacher, seamstress, milliner, school teacher and farmer.

She attended the Moravian School in the "Village" a cluster of houses owned by the Moravian Church west of the Sanctuary. She completed the 6th grade there. At one time she also took classes along with the Pastor's children on the third floor of the Manse, the pastor's residence.

Her mother died when she was 11 or 12 years old. As the second of seven children born to Harry and Lillian Samuel, she took on the responsibility of raising her siblings under her grandmother's supervision.

MUSICIAN

She was a talented musician, who was taught by Mrs. Penn, who had been taught by her mother. Harry Marsh gave her an organ and at the age of twelve, she was playing the organ at the Emmaus Moravian Church. She played there until Rev. Barrow came in 1930.

Miss Ella, as she was known by many, became the organist at the Lutheran Church when Carl Francis was pastor and played there until the 1970's. Her father had white horses and she used to ride one to Cruz Bay when she went there to play the organ at church She also played at the Methodist Church in St. John for a while when it was newly established. During the 1980's Miss Ella returned to Emmaus as organist and director of the Young Adult Choir.

When she gave piano lessons, for some reason her male students were the ones who excelled with the exception of Mrs. Genevieve Moorehead. Among them were Guy Benjamin, Elroy Sprauve, and Dave Matthias. All three have played organ and piano in their respective churches. Guy Benjamin who lived nearby and remained a good friend was just 2½ years younger than his teacher.

SEAMSTRESS

Miss Ella remembers the Sewing Project that started at Harrisburg, one of her father's houses, with Mrs. Penn. As time went by, she ended up sewing dresses for ladies in the community, including Pastor's wives like Mrs. Penn. Long ago, she would sew all night sometimes and would receive $1.25 for a dress. Later, it would be $2.00, $2.50, $2.75. She made boys' shirts, men's underwear — all kinds of things.

As Director of the Sewing Project, she supervised about nine people. This program, a Division of the V.I. Department of Welfare was located for many years at Carolina and Calabash Boom. Then it started in Cruz Bay. Miss Ella worked at all three places. Material came from St. Thomas and went to Miss Gerda Marsh at Carolina. The seamstresses sewed on treadle machines—Singer "foot" machines. To embroider or do fancy work one had to regulate a screw under the machine.

She would do all the cutting of the clothing that was made for school children and the elderly. This cutting was done free-hand. Although no patterns were used at first, the clothes fit very well. Some time later, paper patterns accompanied the fabric. It was such a productive staff that they made clothes for children in St. Thomas and St. Croix also. They began to make school uniforms in 1962.

Some of the ladies who worked for the Sewing Project sewed at home. Among them were Louise Sewer at East End; Doris Samuel, in Coral Bay, and some people in Cruz Bay. Miss Ella would send cut material for a few seamstresses to sew until they learned to cut fabric on their own.

Miss Ella's Singer treadle machine.

Photo: Warren Wells, Jr.

The Fashion Emporium

Polka Dot Match
$2.00

Checked Bolero
$2.75

Cool Tiny Prints
$2.25

Crish Cotton Suit
$0.89

Cool Summer Suit
$1.90

Cid's Wonderland

Courtesy of The Daily News, June 21, 1940.

MILLINER

Not content to be a proficient seamstress or talented musician, Miss Ella decided to continue her education and increase her income by enrolling in a millinery course. She completed it and obtained a degree from the Louie Miller International School of Millinery on July 8, 1949. She created felt and straw hats as well as tams.

TEACHER

Miss Ella taught at the first nursery school in St. John in the Pastory area close to where the first Jehovah's Witness Church was located. She worked with Mrs. Huldah Sewer who went on to teach at Julius E. Sprauve School.

Never one to be idle, she became a substitute teacher at the Horace Mann School in John's Folly, Coral Bay and Bethany School in Cruz Bay. Then through the foster grandparents program from about 1980 to 1987, she taught at the Benjamin Franklin, later renamed Guy H. Benjamin School.

FARMER

During her farming period she raised cows, goats, and pigs. She said that "Hypolite Brin (a butcher in St. Thomas) would go through my flock himself and pay on the spot for animals and I would keep them until he was ready. In those days, Mr. Lockhart of St. Thomas had Holstein cows at his estate in St. John. Mr. Marsh had Zebu in Carolina, St. John and I had Red Poll. They were all red with no horns. There were over 20 cows in my flock."

GROCERY CLERK

Once when Miss Ella worked in a shop in Cruz Bay, she recalls selling some goat meat and didn't realize at the time that it had come from her own flock of goats.

Red Poll

Photo courtesy of
Dan and Mary Jo Schniesing,
St. Henry, Ohio

DESCENDANTS

Although she accomplished much in her life, Ella Hodge would probably consider her family to be her proudest achievement. Her only child, Yvonne and son-in-law Warren Wells, Sr. have made her the grandmother of three children—Warren Jr., Dionne and Maurice. They in turn have given her several great-grandchildren whom she enjoyed baby-sitting.

Miss Ella (as St. Johnians called her, even though she was a Mrs.), also known as Ella Jane, was the second of nine children born to Lillian and James "Harry" Samuel. She gained three more siblings from his second marriage to a schoolteacher, also named Ella.

She worked in the Virgin Islands Government in various capacities, was an entrepreneur, and served as organist for three churches: Emmaus Moravian, Nazareth Lutheran and St. John Methodist.

Her only daughter, Yvonne, and only granddaughter, Dionne, followed in her teacher's footsteps, becoming teachers themselves with both moving up the ranks to serve as Principal of the Guy H. Benjamin and Julius E. Sprauve Schools and Superintendent of Education for the St. Thomas/St. John School District.

With her activity-packed life, perhaps her best legacy is her fine parenting skills. We might ask, "Where did she find the time to be a good mother and grandparent?" Miss Ella showed that hard work just makes one stronger by living to be 100 years old.

Naomi Jacobs
September 15, 1921 – December 6, 2012

In front of the cook house
at Annaberg

Naomi Jacobs with baskets, wist reed, and brooms, in front of Emmaus Moravian Church, Coral Bay

Photo: Tony Scimeca

INTERVIEW AT HER HOME by her daughter, Janet Burton.

JB: What was it like growing up in St. John, Ma?

SUNDAYS

NJ: Growing up in St. John when I was a child was very different to how it is today. The first thing, the first day of the week, Sunday, the whole family would go to church. My father used to sing in the choir and after a while some of his children sang in the choir also. [Her father, John Prince, earned ten cents a day as a laborer on Estate Carolina, but left work at mid-day on Friday to attend choir practice.]

Sundays, people used to visit friends, relatives and members of the church. Even the minister used to do visiting sometimes, not on Sunday, but during the week. And the minister used to have Sunday School in the villages. They used to have Sunday School Mary's Point, Bordeaux, John's Folly, and East End. You see the ministers don't go out in village today.

SCHOOL DAYS

NJ: When I got a little older and I started to go to school, our school wasn't that very big so I being in the first grade some of us had to stay back and go to school half day, so I only went half day from 12:30 to 3:00pm.

[*My mother used to have to stay with a babysitter named Mary Hendricks during the morning since she had to leave home at the same time as her older sisters and brother.*] I asked her if lunch was from 12 to 12:30pm. She said, "What lunch? We didn't have any lunch. Our parents used to give us a piece of bread to carry to school. We didn't have any homework to take home.

The teacher would put the lesson on the board and we would copy it and we would do all our work at school. It was very far different to what it is today.

JB: What are some of the ways that going to school was different to how it is now?

NJ: Well, the first thing I would think on is the American flag. And I always say that I don't know what big thing they are making about the American flag now because I know when I used to go to school you had to pledge allegiance to the flag and after that you had your prayers to say. In fact you never run in in school like … It's hardly worth talking about these thing nowadays because this is something below any kind of degree. If I had to rate it, they will get a big, big, zero.

JB: Well let us know how it was when YOU went to school.

NJ: Well the first thing I must say that the children weren't like now. That the teachers weren't like now. Because the children were willing to learn the lesson and the teachers were willing to teach and they used to help. And you couldn't be rude in school. We didn't know about being rude like today. But one thing I know is that long ago although things were hard, still the people were willing to learn, they were more behaved and everything.

And I think one of the reasons for that too was you get what you deserve. And the children, for instance, you had to walk to school. You had to get up and get ready in the morning, eat whatever you had to eat, had chores to do and you would be there for when the bell ring. Because if you are not there when the bell ring you going to surely miss some of your lessons. So no children would want to be walking in there late, you had games to play and things like that. The one good thing about it was that every holiday, national holiday, although we were not living in America, but because we were, you would say, territories or whatever you want to call it, we would celebrate these holidays: Washington birthday, Lincoln Birthday, Memorial

Naomi Prince's sixth grade
school report card

Basketry

Day, Thanksgiving Day, all these days you would observe. And we used to look forward to these holidays and it used to give a break in the schools and help to teach you to not being afraid to speak to people and things like that because you always had recitations and songs to sing.

JB: You had kindergarten?

NJ: No it didn't have kindergarten when I started to go to school. And these are some of the things that we used to look forward to. When I told someone about a month or two ago about the first flag, Betsy Ross, and Washington, they don't know anything about these things. You know. And I want to know where was the American Flag all the time. Where it was? So, I always have to come back like a minister on the text because we were before our time. That's how it seemed to me for true, you know. Because when Papa used to sing the song about "Let's take a trip in the airship" I wish I had know that song. It had end "and visit the man in the moon." So some of the things the people had foresight. They have the big planes and thing now flying. From when, that was the Wright Brothers? See how long that is! And they had it in the mind to fly. I mean they only improve on it, improve on it, improve on it. But this isn't something that they just start now.

JB: How old were you when you finished school?

NJ: I think they have 13 on the thing [report card].

JB: What grade did you go to?

NJ: Six. We only had as far as sixth grade in those days.

JB: And this was at the Benjamin Franklin School?

NJ: Yes.

JB: Now, I just want to go back to a couple things that you mentioned before. When you said that your parents gave you lunch to take to school, did you have a lunch box?

NJ: What we used to have, our parents used to sew a little bag and give us our lunch to take in the bag. Put a string to the top and you could pull it like some of the purse that you see around.

AGRICULTURE

We used to get plenty of rain. We used to grow most of the food that we eat. We had cows we used to milk. We baked our own bread. My brother used to make baskets. As a matter of fact, when I came from school, got out of school, I used to make wist reed which I'm still doing up to now. That was one of the things that most of the people in St. John used to do at that time and then they used to send them over to St. Thomas to the Cooperative.

JB: OK. You remember who used to milk the cows?

NJ: Well, another sister, Ophelia, and myself used to milk the cows when our father go out early to work. We used to go in the pasture, chase out the cows, take them for water, draw water, and tie the calves and next morning we get up and we milk the cows. We had milk to make butter, banacleva and sometimes when we cook cereal we cook it with pure milk.

We had different kinds of fruit trees. And all this was up Johnny Hone. We had mangoes, sugar apples, custard apples, mamey apples, we had cashews—red and white, soursops and kenneps (genips), you name it we had it.

JB: Guavas,

NJ: Right. Guavaberries were the only things we didn't have up there, but we had over on the other place over Saunders Gut.

JB: Any avocadoes?

NJ: Not in my time, but it had before.

JB: Mesples?

NJ: No, I don't remember mesples.

JB: So since we were on the topic of food, I don't think we said too much about the gardens that people had long ago, they used to call them a "ground"? Could you say a little bit about grandfather's or granny's grounds?

NJ: Yes, we used to have bananas. He had to cut a bunch in two, they were so big. They used to grow up here on the hillside of Carolina above Miss Gerda Marsh's house.

NJ: Yeah. And a kerosene tin of tannias was $2, I think. We had sweet potatoes, pigeon peas, cassava, pumpkins. I don't think we had a lot of melons, but people used to grow melons and pineapple, you name it, we had a lot of food. And sometimes, mostly Christmas time and Easter time or so, not too very often they would kill a calf. We used to eat more goat meat and still not a lot of that. The people never used to eat a lot of meat in those days and that was the reason why probably they never get some of these

JB: diseases, sicknesses.

NJ: Yeah.

JB: I guess that's why they were so healthy because they ate a little bit of meat, lots of fish

NJ: They did a lot of walking

JB: lots of fruit and vegetables, and the starches that they ate were mostly vegetable, fresh vegetables. They walked long distances.

NJ: Because they used to grow cabbage, and tannia bush, and some of those things. We used to eat a lot of kallaloo. And even to some what we don't eat like bata bata and so some of the people put in kallaloo and thing too. But okras and things like that? Yeah, man.

JB: And everything was fresh, nothing was frozen, nothing was canned.

NJ: No, and

JB: About the only thing you would do to preserve things would be to dry them or to put salt in them.

NJ: They used to have fresh coffee. Coffee and cocoa.

Calabash Tree

JB: Where did the coffee and cocoa grow? What part of the island?

NJ: It had Bordeaux. I think there's a cocoa tree still Cinnamon Bay. There were some on Mr. Gerhardt Sprauve's property in Adrian.

NJ: We used to make cocoa tea. On Sunday, my father used to stir the egg and then he used to have the coffee with his milk. And one thing I didn't say too, we used to make cassava bread. He said when he was growing up, his family only used to eat flour bread on Sunday, but they ate a lot of cassava bread.

Calabashes

Sometimes I have been saying I should grate a cassava and wring it and make cassava dumpling. You see, if you had other people with you, but you one sometimes …

There are different kinds of cassava. The bitter cassava is the one that Papa used to have. Maybe you could use the sweet one too. The bitter one had big roots and I believe the bitter cassava was bigger than the other. They used to call it bittersweet.

We used to eat a lot of cassava bread and you would put it in fresh cow's milk. Mama [Helen Prince] never made cassava bread. It was Aunt Louisa Biel who used to bake cassava bread.

We used to make our own breads. And especially at Confirmation Time we would have lots of cakes and according to what season it was we would have rice pudding or sometimes we might have pone, made with sweet potatoes and "punkin". And we varied the things according to the season, the time of the year. And we send out to our people, in those days it was more or less like bartering. You didn't have much money and so people used to exchange.

Sometimes you used to have a lot of visitors and especially according to what time of the year it was. Mostly at Christmas time you would have more than any other time.

FISHING

My father had a boat which he used to keep, sometimes Leinster Bay, or sometimes Brown's Bay. And one of our cousins used to work at Leinster Bay, Alfred Christian, and sometimes we used to go Mary's Point moonlight night to look for lobster.

NJ: We used to go with George Sewer to Maysay Bottom and thing looking for lobster when we had moved down from Johnny Hone to Zootenval.

NJ: They used to come out to feed in the night. Bert Prince, my nephew, was the last one I've been out with looking for anything and that was crab. So they would want to know where we used to get our food, but we never used to spend all this money.

I know when Alec [Alexander Dalmida] them, he was my mother godchild, and they used to send corned hardnose and bonito fish from Bordeaux and they must be used to get apple or something in return. The Bordeaux men used to fish Lameshur Bay. Philip O'Connor used to sell fish Coral Bay. Walter Dalmida and Winfield Matthias used to fish too.

JB: When grandfather caught the fish what did he do with them? Did you eat all of them? Because in those days I'm sure people used to catch a good many fish.

NJ: We had no frigidaire to put any in so he used to pull trap sometimes four times a week. Monday, Wednesday, Friday and Saturday. And he used to sell big strap of fish for 10 cents. Ha! Ha!

JB: What were some of the other sea foods you had besides fish and lobster?

NJ: Whelks and conch.

JB: How you used to get the conch?

NJ: You could walk out sometimes and they used to be right near the surf of the sea. You didn't have to dive for conch and whelks. Sometimes when you go to pick the whelks you hardly wet your feet and they are right there on the stones.

JB: Could you tell about the time when you and Aunt Ophelia were picking whelks?

NJ: When I went back for the donkey?

JB: Yeah, yeah.

NJ: Man deyn want all a dah.

JB: Yes, I want it.

NJ: You want it, well you put it then.

JB: It's better if you tell it.

NJ: They'll say people were glus.

JB: Nooo.

NJ: That time with the whelks, yeah, we went from Bass Hill down and

JB: to Brown's Bay?

NJ: Yeah, the whelks were there on the stones [this was before the National Park owned that property] they were telling you "Come pick me."

JB: And a whole lot of them

NJ: The whelks were there calling us. So the only thing we could do is leave my sister [Ophelia] there and I go back for the donkey and the down boxes.

NJ: But I don't think that was better than the time Ralph and I went to Battery beach at Fortsberg. It was an Easter Monday over here ... and it was calm, calm, calm and all we was doing was stooping down and picking up those big horseshoe whelks. They were brown.

And crabs? They used to be knocking us down on the road. Across Annaberg. So we used to have to go pick them up out the road. They used to be inviting us to pick them.

RECYCLING

I does tell them when I talking to them Annaberg that you didn't have plastic, you didn't have these pile of

Pampers, these pile of cans and bottles. We never used to have it and I does tell them that we used to recycle. And it isn't any lie. You had to save your container. People wasn't buying like 6 lbs. ah thing. In those days I don't know how much you used to buy, maybe a half pound and a pound of these things. But you had to carry your container to get your butter, your lard, your oil. You didn't have these soda can. You never see garbage knocking around the place. I have tell some of the white people they should have been here at that time when St. John was clean. That's the truth. These disease and thing I believe a lot coming from pollution.

MONEY

They didn't have a pile of money, but they were happier than people are today. Money can't make a person happy.

JB: Well, I guess the more you have, the more you have to worry about.

NJ: Well,

JB: If you have nothing to steal you wouldn't worry about a robber.

NJ: Exactly. And the people in those days had nothing to steal or they didn't feel like people would steal because they never even used to lock their house.

JB: I don't think they owned locks. They probably didn't have such a thing as a lock.

NJ: Well, maybe, a stone could ah do the job. [Some persons put a stone to keep the door closed, while others used a hook fastened in a staple.]

GOING TO ST. THOMAS

JB: Yes, I like to hear about the St. Thomas trips.

NJ: Well, going to St. Thomas we never used to pay the boat. It was a free trip. Because you go to St. Thomas, you get a free passage on the boat, you go to one of your family or friends, you eat and drink and you come back home, so whatever little money you make, whether from handicraft or animals, or eggs or chickens, whatever, that was yours. And they would take [buy] things sometimes from the merchants in St. Thomas like Elliot Thomas. I know my father used to take things from him. Every Christmas you were sure you were going to get a ham free. Today don't care how much money you spend, you don't get a ham. So the days were still better than now because you were sure of a ham. That was how people used to live. And I do believe that was the African way, you know. You don't think so?

JB: Sharing and giving?

NJ: Yeah.

JB: Maybe, maybe that's where it came from.

GOING TO TORTOLA

JB: Did you make any trips to other islands besides St. Thomas?

NJ: Yes. I made a trip to Tortola. I don't know how old I must have been when I started going to Tortola. But I know I made quite a few trips on the sailboat to Tortola. That's when things were very, very cheap. You could get a heap of potatoes for ten cents. You weren't getting plenty money but things were cheap.

JB: So you would go to Tortola to shop? Why?

NJ: We used to go to the doctor. I think fifty cents or something we used to pay the doctor, you know.

JB: So while you were there you did a little shopping or so before you came home?

NJ: Yeah, we used to go to the dentist up there too, because you couldn't go St. Thomas unless. I don't know of many boats that would have gone to St. Thomas and come back the same day. They would have had to be a fast boat. You might have been able to do it from the north side but not from Coral Bay.

ABOUT BOATS

JB: So when the boats ... you mentioned the men from East End when there was a west wind they would go to St. Thomas just for the fun of it and come back because they said it wasn't every day you'd get a wind like that. Would they be coming back the same day or was it another day?

NJ: Well, I think they would have gone around East End and then go down the Gut.

JB: To Red Hook?

NJ: Well I don't know how far. They mightn't have gone all the way down to St. Thomas and then they would have come up on the South. Sometimes, especially if it calm it might take nearly a whole day to get to St. Thomas and I know when they had the Second Worlds War it was in '43? They had a gate in St. Thomas and 6 o'clock they would close the gate and if you go after 6pm you have to sleep outside [the harbor].

JB: So you ever had to sleep outside in a boat?

NJ: No. I don't think too many people had to. But I know people have had to sleep outside there. And then they would open it, I don't know whether 6 o'clock or when the next morning, but what happened was too that I think Caneel Bay boat used to bring the mails or something like that so they would open for that. Yeah. It's strange that, you know, they talking about what it is they does say? About the place in case of this and in case of that

JB: Disaster?

NJ: Yeah, but I don't know if they have anything like a gate that they could put up in case

JB: Terrorism, you mean?

NJ: Yeah, yeah. Because these are things that people do, you know so ... I tell you we were before our time.

SPORTS

JB: What kind of games did you play as a child?

NJ: We never used to play much games, apart from rounders in school. They never used to play too much in school.

JB: Rounders?

NJ: Yeah. Miss Gerda Marsh them. It have had women team playing cricket and things like that. But we weren't in it.

JB: I think one of your sisters at one time used to play cricket.

NJ: Laura. She should know what it is.

JB: But you used to play pick-up by yourself.

NJ: Oh yeah. You know when I was Johnny Hone the day I was playing pick-up? I was looking to see if I couldn't still play pick-up and I tell Ralph, I say, anytime you see Indi [Ralph Prince's granddaughter, India] putting stone on the back of her hand you will know what it is. But all that you see, children used to do. Not today.

JB: How about parties?

NJ: We used to go East End to family parties. Christmas time.

JB: At whose house? Who had the parties?

NJ: Cousin Maud Harley. It used to be to Cousin Maud house. I must say that my grandfather, my one grandfather was from East End, so we had a lot of family from East End.

JB: What was your mother like?

NJ: Well, my mother, she liked to stay at home. I guess and family come and visit. Sometimes she used to iron clothes for different people, as far as I know. What she used to do was taking care of us when we were small and she liked to go in the garden to reap. She used to cook and bake bread and you know?

JB: She was a regular housewife.

NJ: Yeah. Washed her husband clothes and things like that.

WASH DAY (LAUNDRY)

JB: What was wash day like?

NJ: Oh, wash day wasn't like now. That was a big day when wash day come, you used to wash out your clothes first before you put the soap on them

JB: You used to wash them without soap?

NJ: Yeah, yeah, you could wash them out without soap. It depends on what kind of work they doing, you know. Suppose you were burning charcoal and things like that. And then you would soap up the clothes and then you would put them to boil. The most of the clothes probably could have taken boiling in those days.

The bath pan was used for bathing and washing clothes

JB: Because of the material of the clothing?

NJ: Right

JB: Cotton and so forth.

NJ: Yeah. And don't forget they used to starch and iron even sheets and pillowcases.

JB: So after the clothes were boiled, what was the next stage?

NJ: Well you wash them out and you rinse them.

JB: So that was the fourth water that they went into.

NJ: Some of the times.

JB: The blueing would be in the rinsing water.

NJ: Right.

JB: You would starch them after they were dry or when they were still wet?

NJ: You could do it both ways, but most time the clothes used to be dry when they starching because not all the time they would starch them the same day either.

JB: So all the clothes were ironed.

NJ: Yes, and they never had these kind of material like …

JB: Polyester

JB: And this was using the coal goose?

NJ: Yeah. Charcoal.

BEFORE E-MAIL

JB: You mentioned the mail boat and so I was thinking about mail because nowadays I think mail comes from St. Thomas to Cruz Bay twice a day to go into the post office boxes. And I was wondering what the mail situation was like when you were growing up, how people got mail, and like how much mail they would get, what sort of mail they would get.

NJ: Well, people still used to get mails, not as often as now. But I know people used to order from this Walter Field catalog, that I know. Sears Roebuck go back a long way too.

JB: There was also one named Aldens.

NJ: Yeah. But Walter Field, a lot of people used to order from Walter Field, C.O.D. [Cash on Delivery].

JB: Everything was C.O.D.?

NJ: Yeah. That was delivery.

JB: Where was the post office in Coral Bay?

NJ: It didn't have no post office in Coral Bay. Mails used to go to Miss Gerda grocery store.

JB: But you don't know where it went before that?

NJ: I think that might have been the first place.

JB: Just on Saturdays you would get mail? At first?

NJ: I think mail used to come up twice a week. I remember one time when Mr. Simmons was Administrator that he sent up the government boat. It had so much packages. I used to work Carolina then. It had so much

A coal goose was used to iron sheets, pillowcases and most articles of clothing

packages and thing that he sent the boat with the mail up here Coral Bay.

JB: That must have been Christmas?

NJ: Yeah. Christmas time.

My brother, Herman Prince, used to bring a lot of packages from Cruz Bay. That when he retire and Mrs. Eudora Marsh, the school Principal, gave this address she said either he was the village father or the village grandfather. Because he had these packages to the side of the horse and thing when he coming from Cruz Bay. But many people used to rely on him to do business for them in Cruz Bay when he go down there to teach basket and thing. But that was how the people used to live. It was like birds of one feather at that time and you flock together. But now it seems, you know, now it's different. But those days will never come back again. They can't.

JB: No.

EMPLOYMENT AND SALARIES

JB: What about the places where YOU worked. The different jobs that you had.

NJ: Well, I worked right here in Coral Bay. I worked to Miss Gerda, I worked to Mr. Sprauve [Julius Sprauve's grocery], I worked at the school.

Naomi at Annaberg with fellow basket maker, Felicia Caines

JB: But what were some of the salaries that you made, for example how much money did you make when you were working at Miss Gerda's store?

NJ: I think it was $15 a month.

JB: And then you said it went to $18. And then you went to the [Benjamin Franklin] school. Oh, you worked for Mr. Sprauve before the school?

NJ: I can't be had work there long [at Mr. Sprauve's].

JB: You remember any salaries you had at the school?

NJ: I told you sometime, but that was when you were in school [college]. I told you why I vote for the Mortar and Pestle. Because I was getting $69 a month. Then it went through (a law was passed) that nobody must get less than $100 a month.

JB: Which is $1200 a year. And they recently passed a law that you can't get less than $15,000 a year. In 2006, I believe it increased to $20,000.

NJ: Yeah?

JB: Mm Hm

NJ: And George Sewer was getting $95 a month so he got $5 raise. Well, money, I mean, getting the money ain't the thing it's what you do with the money because some people get lots of money and they have nothing to show for it and some get a lil bit of money and they still have something to show for it.

A table mat of wist, whose design Naomi copied from a doily made by crochet

JB: So you worked at Benjamin Franklin Elementary School as a cook. Where else did you work? I know you had one or two part-time jobs after you retired from the school.

NJ: After I retired from the school, Oh, oh, Annaberg.

JB: Long ago, if you didn't order clothes from the Walter Field catalog, a seamstress would make them for you. Once you told me about Easter dresses that were made for you and your sisters.

NJ: Well, you remember Marie Penn? She lived at Miland.

I had to go for the dresses one Sunday morning from Johnny Hone. When I got to Cow Pen I went through Number Two as a shortcut. I had to pick up the clothes and get back home in order to make it to church for 11:00 o'clock service.

When Pauline and Ophelia were working Caneel Bay, I used to ride the donkey and carry bread, tart, etc. for them. Once when I was passing Cinnamon Bay, Clifford Smalls gave me green bananas, limes, etc. In those days, fellows were not fresh. They never bothered you.

Large and medium-sized mats, coasters, a sandwich tray and bread tray made from wist — a locally grown vine

NAOMI'S FAVORITE SAYINGS:

1. *We don't drag our chair.* (If they want you to visit they'll invite you.)

2. *They'n gon' dance on my head.* (They are not going to have a good time off me.)

3. *When the ministers come here to eat, the lady does go haygay haygay to sit with them.*

4. *I don't see why* (insert name) *have to let people dig dey eye out dey head.*

5. *When wind blow yo see fowl bottom. When you stir up shit yo smell it.*

6. *Maybe I would have visited her already, but when you hear about these big mantwana house …*

7. (insert name) *must have cursed the hour damn the minute that she started organizing the Senate.*

8. *Emmaus is "Come go see."* (You have to see it to believe it!)

9. *These people eating tart like five and 40.* (They are eating it fast.)

10. *He know he could blow wind in* (insert name) *face and send him to sleep.* (He could control him.)

11. *Bleck.* (Good-for-nothing) *Thundering bleck.* (worse than a bleck)

12. *Mary Smith* (Naomi's grandmother) *wasn't no two-cent baby.*

13. The Folklife Festival needed volunteers. *"You see that's where these Senators who runnin' should a been tic a tang wid it."*

14. *Look how she kapelling!* (The pot of ginger and cinnamon was boiling up good.)

15. *When turkey wing broke they does rank with fowl.*

16. *Bernie know he and I can't set hass* (horse). (We don't get along.)

17. *Water boilin' for fish, fish don' know.*

18. (Insert name) *neither has a stick standing nor a feather flying.* (Someone who cannot help another person, someone who is destitute)

19. *But the man look so salah* (emphasis on the second syllable). *I look at him dey other day and the man had neider bottom nor belly.*

20. *Goat head and sheep head ain't one.* (What they do for one ain't mean they gon' do that fo another.)

21. *When yo see dey give St. John anything, yo must know it is some kind of winggay thing. I does say all kind of winggay thing.*

22. *Joseph must be gon come up today, but then he can't be does postar with Emmaus. He must be does postar with Bethany.* (bother with)

23. *Smelling up roun' people* (When you want something from people)

24. *Lallup* (When yo can't keep from somebody)

25. He (Jonathan) always talking *folaygn* talk. (nonsense)

26. *What a kallaloo with the bower. Bower*—stalks, etc. Cook the whole bush instead of the leaves only. (*What a mash-up!*)

27. *She must be have to bite and blow.* (She has to keep her mouth shut. Can't talk about or say how she feels about a matter.)

28. *Buh dem out dey laughin' like a parcel a asses.* (John Prince referring to his three daughters out in the kitchen). Some people (like John Prince) built their kitchens separate from the house.

29. *Things come on horseback, but they take their own time to go.*

30. *While some people say he thinny and rahnee bony, he exposin' heself.*

31. *No lawyer ain't gon knock no knife and fork aff of me.*

32.   I'm not clearing ground for monkey to run race.

33.   Joseph could tark lard oil. (Talking over your face. Talking trying to confuse people, without success).

34.   John Prince used to say, "*Give way yo ass, shit through yo ribs.*"

35.   If he think because people is family you gon' let them rub shit in your mouth, he mistaken.

36.   If they think I bahn behind cow bottom, they lie. Let dem wait. (I'm not stupid.)

37.   Lapiass time, as in old old thing from lapiass time.

38.   Thass why yo see he runnin' like fowl hard wid egg ready to drap.

39.   And (insert name) was there today and *she didn't piss on cotton give him to smell.* (She didn't study him. She didn't pay him any attention.)

40.   They gon' have it *ding dong for a dumplin'.* (Some hard going)

41.   John Testamark used to say, "*When bull dead, he leave trouble for he skin.*"

42.   John Prince used to say, "*That's a young twister.*" (Speaking about high winds, e.g. 25+ mph)

43.   (insert name) *ga ting he gon pulperize wid it.* (It's going to spoil.)

44.   John Prince. "*Who put dey ass on the pan will sit down on the blister.*"

45.   The Senior Citizens is *pushy kaka* now. (cat poop) Said after: "We haven't heard about the Senior Citizens Ball this year. (Also means low on the totem pole, of not much esteem)

46.   John Prince to his children: "*Get up early so dey dead people spirits don't walk on you.*"

47.   They mightn't want to say anything, because they might say as yo spit they gan wid it.

48. That's a *commess*. (Speaking about someone's situation with her children having children, in the same house, etc.)

49. Woong woong—half stupid (people got them wooong woong).

50. Suttie—half crazy, not too collective

51. Some people don't have no *santoma* (emphasis on the final syllable). (craw)

52. The same thing that you kick with your foot you have to take up with your hand.

53. The eyes of the master fatten the horse. (If you are around to see what is going on then you do better than if you aren't there.)

54. One lil markament apple (speaking about an apple tree on which I didn't see any apples. There's one lil markament apple on the tree.)

55. If you go down (lose your social standing, for example), people will have more sympathy if you're not *ringkingkish* (proud)

56. Dey does laugh outlaudid. I think it's only black people who does laugh outlaudid.

57. Pashima—inferior, not developed good (accent on the last syllable)

With her older and only brother, Herman, Naomi walked through the St. John bush for over 60 years cutting vines for hoop baskets and other native handicrafts. She would often say the distances they covered would be equal to going from the Virgin Islands to New York and back. Among her other close relatives were her parents: John and Helen Prince, three sisters: Pauline, Laura, and Ophelia; a daughter, Janet, and grandson, Jonathan. She was married to Alphonse Jacobs for over 25 years.

Naomi was a part of Virgin Island National Park's Living History Program at Annaberg, demonstrating basketry and native cooking. She participated as a tradition bearer in the 1991 St. Croix Folklife Festival and the 1996 Folklife Festival in St. Thomas.

Naomi always lived close to the land, planting herbs and trees, especially fruit trees. She knew how to take care of cows, donkeys, goats, pigs, and chickens as a child. She could build and burn a coal pit and knew how to survive without modern conveniences. Her herbal knowledge was used to cure certain ailments instead of going to the doctor for every medical problem. She was an excellent baker and cook who lived her culture daily. Although she appeared to be a quiet person, Naomi was no "two cent baby" and could defend herself very well if she needed to. Throughout her life she had a strong faith in God and served in the Emmaus Moravian Church. Alzheimer's Disease sidelined her in December, 2006.

Leander Rudolph Jurgen
December 11, 1911 – December 20, 1985

By Thecla Jurgen Hanley

Leander Rudolph Jurgen

DADDY LOVED TO SING, dance and play the harmonica. He loved family, he loved God, he loved working in the garden. He loved to dress. He loved farming and he loved making stew [preserves].

MUSIC

My mother, Nerita, played the organ for the Catholic Church and every evening Daddy would have us gather around her and we'd all get a Sankey and sing while she played at least an hour or more of Moravian Hymns. And whenever it was time to quit, Daddy wanted to go on singing some more.

He liked dancing to Quelbes and local songs like that at home. He was excellent at playing the harmonica, and was always a want-to-be guitar player. Couldn't play anything, but had a guitar and would be strumming and not making much sense of that.

CONSTRUCTION WORK

He liked doing masonry and carpentry work around the house and in fact his history in construction began at Caneel Bay, the old K.C. Bay. He started there as a carpenter and told many stories about earning cents in the day working at K.C. Bay. We have a bench home that I refuse to get rid of 'cause he made it.

During retirement, he worked with St. John Lumber Company for five or maybe 10 years and that was in the line of his first love—working with wood.

QUALIFICATION FOR POLICE OFFICER

When he was given the opportunity to join the Police Force he jumped at it. Even though the dollars were very, very few, they were much more than the cents. Daddy said he was hired because of his stature. The interview was just to stand in line and he had the build and they went for it. That's it. That's what they were looking for and he joined.

EDUCATION

Daddy could type. He was honored at one point with a lot of lady secretaries, because he typed for his job before Joan Thomas was hired as his secretary. He taught Cleone Creque Hodge, his niece, many others, and myself to type.

My father took pride in his spelling and math abilities. Always. He attended Bethany Moravian School until 6th grade. But he said no one could spell and do math as well as he could.

ETIQUETTE

I always remember him eating with a fork and knife. The table had to be set with a fork and knife. And many times I would say, "Daddy you eating soup, you don't need a fork and knife!" He would say, "Bring me my fork and knife!" Of course you did that and didn't ask any more questions.

STORYTELLER

He loved to tell long stories when people came to visit. It didn't matter if it was his peers or if it was any of my other siblings' and my age group. We'd all leave the room while our friends were subjected to those stories.

He told stories about his childhood—old time stories, life experience stories. But they would be long and drawn out. Way past you catching the point. If you caught the point and you said, "O.K. I understand", he would still be going on elaborating on those stories.

TOURIST

I remember him going on a tour of the United States with a few other St. Johnians. My aunt Gerda and her husband, Albert Sewer, went with him. I'm not sure how many states he toured, but when he came back he sat and typed ooh a long journal and sent it to everyone he knew. All the family members received copies. He called us up, I guess, to check to see if we read it and would question us about certain parts of his report.

STEWED PRESERVES

Daddy prepared preserves like stewed gooseberry, guava, and tamarind. He'd spend a lot of time in the kitchen preparing those 'cause Mom didn't want any part of that. And he would give to his children's friends or anybody going away [to the States]. He'd give a little jar of stew.

THE HOUSE THAT MOVED

After speaking to my brother, Ken, last night about this interview, he asked me to mention when our family lived in St. Thomas. Ken is my parents' second child, he remembered living in Savan on St. Thomas and spending a lot of time at his grandmother's house on St. John. I think my parents owned a wooden house in Savan on a piece of land that they rented. When they bought some property in the Washington School area, or Haabets Gade, they just moved the whole house, put it up and built around it, then dismantled the original house. Ken said even then back in that day he thought that was kind of strange. But I guess it was a way of cutting costs.

DISCIPLINARIAN

Ken also mentioned that Daddy never spoke about his job or anything having to do with his job. Even when I was grown, I remembered that too. He wouldn't bring home stories about his work. He'd tell stories about his own life. He didn't like kids having guns, owning guns. That was a no-no definitely. You coudn't have a gun for a toy. Ken said, the neighborhood children and their friends were afraid of my father because of his size—he was so tall. They were also afraid of his voice, because he was so stern and strict, a real disciplinarian. People would bring their children by to have him talk to them, and I guess that created a problem.

EMBARRASSMENT FOR LIFE

Daddy was going out to work one evening and Vergil, my eldest brother was hanging with his friends, Gaylord Sprauve and some others. Daddy saw them on the corner and sent Vergil home. He said "It's time for you to go home." Vergil was with his friends and he said "O.K. I'll be going in a little while, Daddy." My father said, "You're going NOW!"

He embarrassed him and Vergil said that's an embarrassment for Life!

YOUTH EMPLOYMENT

Ken said Daddy always insisted that you must have a job or a trade, never be idle. Because of that Ken had to work starting at age 7 and he had many jobs before he reached age 16, including working at a shoe repair, Clinton's paint shop, at Walter Chinnery's supermarket, other supermarkets, Lindquist's Garage, Reed's Movies on St. John, (my brother told me he had to come up because he was working for Mr. Reed in St. Thomas and had to bring movies to St. John to show, I think at the Battery). He worked for V.I. Hotel, but that was many jobs my brother had at home before he was even old enough to hold a job.

POLICE OFFICER ON DUTY

My father rode a three-wheel motorcycle in St. Thomas for the Police Department. I'm not sure if they had vehicles then or what that was about, but his assignment in patrolling the streets of St. Thomas was to patrol it on a three-wheel motorcycle.

Leander Rudolph Jurgen Command

Photo: Janet Burton

He took his job real serious. I remember one time being at the Police Station waiting for him and he looked down the street and saw a tourist all the way down by the intersection without a shirt on and he said, "Don't go anywhere, I'll be right back" and went down to tell the man he had to put on a shirt. Of course that's not something that we insist on now. But Daddy always had his shirt on. He loved to wear that white long-sleeved police shirt, you know the special occasion shirt, of course.

I remember when they were giving the pin, VIPD, and I said "What does VIPD mean?" He said "Very Important Police Department". He put "Important", he didn't say "Virgin Islands". He said "Very Important", I remember that much, "Very Important Police Department."

4TH OF JULY

Back in the day when St. John Carnival Parades were led by the Police Department, policemen, with my father, would march up in front of the parade and lead the parade around the town and then he would stop at the Police Station and the parade would go to the end where it ends now by the bandstand or wherever it ended at that time.

FREE FOOD AT THE POLICE STATION

In those days the police were friends of the people. I remember lots of people hanging around the Police Department, the Police Station, to witness the parade but used the Police Station as a place of relaxation. They'd go in and sit down out of the sun, get water, and use the restroom. My mother prepared food and brought it down so that the people who came by the Police Station could get a free meal. A free mutton and rice, whelks and whatever, conch and whatever—you know the things that you buy now in booths? Those things were free. And I remember my mother preparing and I remember my father asking my aunt Lena Blake also, and they would be cooking these things to bring down to the Police Department. I'm sure other wives or husbands, of the policemen contributed and they did the same. And of course my father would bring a lot of St. Thomian police up to the house and they would come and stay, and they'd get a meal.

YOU CAN'T FOOL ME

When he was sick, on his deathbed, and he was hallucinating from the medication that they were giving him, the family members would spend a lot of time at his bedside and he would say "Thecla, I'm going to Cruz Bay to pick up Bassanio David" (another police officer in St. Thomas). "You want to go down with me?" I'd say, "O.K.", 'cause I'm playing along with him and he'd say "O.K. Get in." So I'd pull the chair closer and he'd say "Girl, that's a chair, get in the car."

AN ARREST

There was an incident when Coral Bay had their festival and Daddy was up in Coral Bay and he had to take in two offenders. But the wrongdoing that they did was taking his hat off his head. One of the persons involved had a discussion with someone else to compare who had better hair, and so the person attempted to remove his hat. I don't know if he mistakenly thought the person was trying to get his gun or something, but he was bringing the people in to Cruz Bay and they tried to attack him in the car to take his gun or to do something in the car and it caused an accident. One or more persons ended up with broken limbs or ribs, something. He was hospitalized. I'm not sure who the individuals were, but I know he was home and that kind of thing. We didn't have real criminals in St. John. I guess that was the big event of the day.

NICKNAMES

Of course, people in St. John would tease him, call him names. Like you know he inherited "Cart Whip" from his father's time because his father was a police officer in St. Thomas and you know that was the name

Leander Jurgen Command
Police Station Plaque

Photo: Janet Burton

they had given him and then after my father grew tall as well and became a police they gave him that title. I remember them calling him Yergie, Yergie Bear (Yogi Bear), and Barney because of Barney Fife, the police officer on the Andy Griffith Show. Yeah, I remember that. I hated it, because I inherited it too. Coming to school the kids would call me those names, you know. And I received a lot of thumps because of the fact that "Well, your father is a police officer" and I'd get a lot of thumps, you know? That comes with the territory, I guess.

ATTEMPTED SABOTAGE

Back in the day wasn't really that bad. We did have some instances where we were, I guess, attacked somewhat. People would come in the yard and mess with the vehicles. I remember someone coming and smashing the windshield of the car. I remember people staying from far areas and firing shots at the house. You would hear the shots and then in the morning you would find the cartridges outside the door. I remember someone once tried to rig his car. He went to get some gas at the gas station and they filled a cup with sand and oil and whatever other chemicals and put it in the gas, rested the cup inside so that when the gas overheated or whatever, it would cause an explosion. St. John streets are so short the car would never overheat going anywhere. So by the time he drove by the next corner he had to stop, that corner he had to stop, whatever, whatever, he stopped at my grandmother's house before he came home and that's where it was discovered. But, it still was safe, still was fairly safe back in the day.

THE CHALK LINE

I remember one 4th of July, my brother Clive was very daring. While my father was in the parade, my brother asked to use the car. My father said, "No." So my brother took the car anyway, and would you know, showing off that he could drive with no hands and not sitting down, he crashed the car. Had it flipped over this hill, going up Caneel Bay Hill, breaking people's arms who were in the car, so … my brother received some lashes. He got spanked, and I remember jumping on the bed and swinging on my father's neck, telling him "Don't hit him! Don't hit him!" Shortly after, Clive was out of here. He left for the States. "Cause he was a child that was not controllable. In fact, I remember my aunt Clarice Thomas talking to my parents complaining Clive saying that he needed to straighten up and walk a straight line (behave properly). And she told him he needed to walk a chalk line. And he took the chalk and drew a line on the ground and walked it. He was just obstinate.

MATURITY

I remember getting this book, *Positive Thinking* by Vincent Peale and I presented my father with the book and told him to read … whatever chapter it was in it about anger. You know, and he said "O.K. and I want you to read it too." I said "I read the whole book." He said, " No, you're going to read that chapter again and then we can sit down and have a discussion. I'm going to read it and you're going to read it and we're going to sit down and discuss it. Hey, you know I felt good because he was willing to listen to my point of view and he was willing to discuss and hear another opinion that did not have to be his way. I told him at the end that was maturity. He said "Maturity for you!"

UNHEALTHY HABIT

As far back as I can remember, Daddy smoked cigarettes. He said he started smoking when he was 11 years old. A year before he died, he had a complete physical and nothing was wrong. The next year a bump grew on his neck and three or four months after that he passed away on December 20th, 1985—the same day as my daughter's birthday.

Captain Jurgen was born to Victor and Mary Jackson Jurgen on St. John, Virgin Islands. He attended the

Bethany School up to the sixth grade, the highest grade on the island at the time.

He joined the Virgin Islands Police Department as a sub-patrolman on January 10, 1942. Between 1944 to 1966 he was promoted six times, attaining the rank of Captain on October 23, 1966.

He retired from the VIPD on November 30, 1971.

Five years later, in 1976, the 11th Virgin Islands Legislature honored him by Resolution No. 811. He received his Retirement Badge during Police Week in 1982.

On May 2, 1983, the Legislature passed a bill to name the St. John Police Station in his honor as the "Captain Leander R. Jurgen Command D." The Dedication Ceremony took place on March 28, 1998 under the administration of Gov. Roy L. Schneider, M.D.

Captain Jurgen was a member of Bethany Moravian Church, a Boy Scout Leader and was involved in the Blood Bank Drive.

Elaine Ione Sprauve

January 9, 1913 – November 23, 1997

Interview of Mr. Elroy Sprauve on October 9, 2001.

JB: Maybe I could get a little bit of information from you about your aunt, Elaine Sprauve—what sort of person she was like, what sort of aunt she was since you were very close to her.

DISCIPLINARIAN

ES: Growing up, we always felt as if we had two mothers because we grew up in the same house with my aunt and my mother. And I should clarify that many people believed that she was my aunt on my father's side, but actually she was my aunt on my mother's side. But she, too, was a disciplinarian. Very firm, but very loving and with her again, education was foremost. I mean, you had to study. She always encouraged you to do well and tried to provide all opportunities to help you to further your studies.

SEE THE GOOD

ES: In those days, for example, if your aunt gave an order it was as if your mother gave an order. My mother would never overrule her. One thing I liked about her up to the day she died she always tried to see the best in people. If you were complaining about somebody, if you were angry with somebody she would listen and then she would always ask you if you could see something good in that person. And she believed it, deep down in her life she actually believed that.

JB: She was a Christian.

ES: Yeah, and she did not admire anyone gossiping. That to her was something she detested. I could always tell when somebody called her on the telephone and was about to gossip. I would hear this silence on the telephone.

JB: She wouldn't encourage them.

ES: She always tried for people to make peace. And always tried to get people to see the best in people.

A NATURAL LEADER

ES: And I don't know where she got the energy from, she was involved in so many different organizations and had leadership roles. But it looked like she thrived on that. This was her forte. She did not relish conversations about cooking or housework. She liked people to talk about organizations, and functions and proactive things in organizations. This was what she really lived for. On the day that she died, she got up the morning and she had a pad just about half an hour before she died, and was telling me she had some things she had to take care of. She always had a yellow pad writing down something.

Elaine Ione Sprauve Library

I remember that when we were growing up as children she was the one who directed the Christmas plays for the church. So we knew that come Christmas time we had to have a part and we had to learn it and learn it well. We had no choice.

JB: I think she was involved in Fourth of July and those kinds of ... .

Elaine Ione Sprauve Library and Museum

TEACHER

ES: Yes. And she was my kindergarten teacher, I remember. She was the first kindergarten teacher in St. John. She was very loving, but very firm. Sometimes people who met her later on would say to me that she was always a pleasant person, and I would say, but she was very firm.

JB: I didn't see that, you know, but I guess if you were around her a lot ...

ES: And especially when it came to anything about school. Schoolwork had to be taken seriously. School and church had to be taken seriously.

JB: One of the things that I really admired about her was her ability to speak so articulately. She was an excellent public speaker. And she spoke without any script. But it seems like she would be able to fit in at any occasion and be able to speak fluently about, just about anything.

PUBLIC SERVANT

ES: I remember even her years working in the Administrator's Office the long hours she would put in, I think her job almost became her commitment to St. John, it was more than a job it was like she was doing it as a commitment to St. John because I remember people would call her at all hours and they would come to her on weekends or after she had a long day at the office. Rather than going up to the office they would come to her house, but she would never get angry or turn them away. And I remember her big concern at the Battery when they were collecting money for the property taxes how sometimes she would go out of her way to contact families and what not when they were falling in arrears just so they would not lose their land.

I think commitment to public service was something that she took very seriously. But then I remember when I came back as an adult and being around her it was such a big change because when we were children we saw her as such a strict disciplinarian and as we got older she was so calm and friendly and we would sit down and talk. Growing up she didn't allow any slack.

[both laugh]

JB: Well, when you came back you were more or less speaking as equals.

ES: Yes! Yes [laughs]

COORDINATOR, ORGANIZER

JB: in a sense ... I remember there was some kind of church service that is celebrated every year. It was a time when all the churches would have people from the congregations participating in this event.

ES: With the women

JB: Women, yes, and she always seemed to be the person who

ES: coordinated it, yes.

JB: was in charge of that. And I don't think it has been as, it hasn't seemed to have the same stature that it did when she was doing it.

ES: She was always coordinating something because I used to laugh sometimes and tell her I think that sometimes she used to make over a hundred telephone calls a day. [laughs] But she was always coordinating something, and getting people to do something to move ahead and do something.

JB: Well, she seems to have been a very organized person.

ES: Yes. Very organized. Very, very organized. She lived for community service. She lived for that. And also what I admire about her, she took painful situations very calmly, regardless of what the situation was she always remained very calm, very poised, [she would] never lose control, or never got into a deep despair, she always seemed [to be able] to pick up and move on. And she took care of so many of her relatives.

JB: I think that sprang from her deep faith, from the Christian life, you might say, that she lived. I mean just looking at it you could see that she was, you know ...

ES: Yes, some of the images I have ... I wish I had that discipline. Even up to the days before she died, every morning, I remember sometimes I would go by her bedroom early, I would always see her kneeling in prayer before her bed. And I always used to admire

Elaine Ione Sprauve's home

Photo: Sprauve Family Collection

that humility. At night before she'd go to bed, in the morning, she used to get down on her knees and pray.

She remained very calm, I think, whenever [there was] anything in the family like any crisis, sickness, death, she was always very collected, very calm, handled it very well.

FAMILY

JB: She just had one sister?

ES: No, she had two sisters. One was Anita Sprauve Joseph and one was my mother.

JB: Any brothers?

ES: Yah, mmhm. She had one brother whose name was. they used to call him Luddie. Ludvig. And he was famous for the guiro. He was mentally handicapped, but he could have played that guiro. I don't know how to do it. He would listen to anybody playing and he could pick up the most difficult rhythm. I don't know if you have seen an old postcard. There was one with Warren Smalls. It's in many old pictures. There's Warren Smalls, Herman Sprauve, Basil Harley and him.

JB: Four musicians.

ES: Yes. That was the only brother that she had. She had one who died as an infant. Some day ago I was saying it was strange that the one sister who was my mother was born on the 9th of April, she [Elaine] was born on January 9th so you had the 9th's there. And the other sister died on May 23rd , and she died on November 23rd. So they had the 23rd's and the 9th's.

UNOFFICIAL ADMINISTRATOR

And of course I think she knew almost everybody on St. John. She came in contact with them in so many ways through the Administrator's Office.

JB: I think many people actually felt that she was the Administrator

ES: Yes! [laughs]

JB: Because she knew the job so well and did it so … if there was no Administrator, no one would have known because the work would have

ES: continued. I think they didn't feel threatened at all going to speak to her.

JB: Would that have been a political job? An exempt position?

ES: No it was not.

JB: Because I was going to say she had worked through many different administrations.

ES: Briefly she served as Acting Administrator. One time Governor King asked her to be Administrator, but she didn't want the position. She told me she would do it for a while. I think she did it for about three or four months.

JB: It probably would have interfered with all the other things that

ES: Oh yes, she wanted to do.

And I don't think she would have liked being in a position that had any sort of control because of political overtones. I don't think she would have wanted that. I don't think she saw any politics in the job at all. She saw she had a job to do to serve the people and many people at that time, I think that's what they saw. They didn't want to get involved in machinations.

JB: What I'm beginning to see is that people of her time seemed to have a lot of principles and integrity and so forth.

ES: And I think this idea of serving people or extending yourself to others was so ingrained in many St. John people at that time. Again I think of Miss Thomas, she brought this message: "You have some obligation to St. John and its people." She said it to us as students, again when we were working with her as adults, the message was still there very, very clear.

JB: I think, even in your time and mine, we still saw ourselves in a certain way as ambassadors …

ES: Yes, yes.

JB: that you wouldn't want to do things that would reflect badly on St. John.

ES: Exactly, exactly. And I find, too, that people had a way of appreciating any effort you put out. I always tell people, too, that I can recall the first Sunday I played in church. Even if I had made a hundred bad notes those old ladies came and they made you feel as if you had done the greatest thing. There was no criticism, well you made a mistake, there was very positive reinforcement. And I think that is something that we have lost. And maybe that's why sometimes we don't have people going into certain positions.

JB: I see an effort along those lines was made in education when students write. Their teachers don't correct all the mistakes they make.

ES: I remember, too, years ago even like in Coral Bay in the Moravian Churches here and in the Lutheran Church like Christmas time if a child recited well, I mean right away they heaped praises on that child.

JB: I think it's something we have lost.

ES: I think now we are very quick to criticize and we don't realize that that has a negative feeling and it keeps people away from coming forward.

Austin Walters said that Auntie Laine was brighter than all the St. John Administrators with whom she worked.

Her daughter (and only child), Jean Nicholson Gibbs, said —

> *"My mother was stern. She knew what she expected of me and didn't hide it. She expected me to be respectful, caring. Her stern talking was enough.*
> *She was overly kind as a person. She would go out of her way, would deny herself to please someone else. She wasn't an envious person. She never said, 'I wish I had…', but was always satisfied with what she had and was willing to share with her family. She preferred to give, not receive. She would make tea for her landscaper and sit and talk with him. She didn't care for public adulation, attention.*

She loved church dearly. She reminded people of every-thing, covering even the smallest details. My mother would make sure the members of her family were going to church, being confirmed, and she would call their parents and follow up. She was a humble person, praying twice a day, always on her knees at the foot of her bed wherever she was.

As a career woman, she was an excellent organizer, fair, and committed to a fault. Whatever task she took on she would do her best."

Miss Sprauve served from the 1940's to 1980 as Customs Clerk, Immigration Officer, Administrative Clerk, Administrative Assistant, and Acting Administrator, at the Battery in St. John.

Julius E. Sprauve, Sr.
March 26, 1893 – May 27, 1965

Julius E. Sprauve, Sr.
portrait

Interview of Elroy Sprauve on October 9, 2001.

PARENTAL DISCIPLINE

ES: O.K. Well, I think I will speak about my father, not so much as a public official, but some memories of growing up with him … and I know my brothers and I, sometimes we would like to joke because he was a disciplinarian, but his method of discipline was not conventional in the sense he did not believe in corporal punishment. But whenever you did something wrong you had to kneel before him and then he would usually quote something from the Bible. And usually it was from the Book of Proverbs. And after he gave a little sermon on that passage from the Bible, then he'd usually tell you something like either that you had to go and clean the yard or you had to go to bed at a very early hour, earlier than usual. I remember one time I got a punishment and I don't think I had done anything bad, but Mr. Richard Ellington was running against him and I wrote some quotation from Julius Caesar on the poster and Sgt. Brown was the police officer. He saw us and we did not see him and he came and I think maybe he was trying to scare us more than anything else, but he came and took us to our father and said we were defacing this poster. And we thought that maybe our father would go easy with us because this man was running against him. But he didn't see that, he figured we had to be punished because we did something wrong. And I always remember that the punishment was during the summer around August and the punishment that we had to be in bed by 4 o'clock in the afternoon. [laughs]

JB: Oh my goodness! That was severe punishment!

ES: [laughs] And of course you know, hearing all the children playing and you in bed by 4. Of course we had to get the lecture from the Bible why we were being punished because we had done something wrong.

Many people saw him as a public official, but up to now, I don't see him as a public official. I remember him as this quiet disciplinarian. He never believed in corporal punishment, but you had to get a lecture, kneel down and get a lecture and then maybe some duty, some task you had to perform. And I found, I would have preferred many times to get a whipping than to go through the lecture.

And I remember him clearly when he had the Estate Sieben, [pronounced seeven] when he had the home out there, sometimes he would just get up one morning and say, "I am sending you all out to Sieben this morning.

NIGHTLY PRAYERS

And another thing, too, we always remember about him is that always until we were confirmed usually by the age of 14, every night you had to say your prayers so he could hear it. And if you had fallen asleep and he waked you up and said, "Did you say your prayers?", even though you said "Yes, father, I said my prayers." He would say, "Say it again, so I can hear it."

JB and ES laugh.

JB: If he didn't hear it, you didn't say it.

ES: You didn't say it. And after you said your prayers you could not talk. So I remember that sometimes we would be there whispering, whispering, whispering because once you said your prayers, with him it was no talking. And I remember too, with him regardless if you didn't have anything to do you had to get up early in the morning. I remember sometimes if you slept past 6 o'clock he would always say, "From the time God make morning!" And sometimes you had nothing to do but you had to get up. He figured it was being slothful to remain in bed say beyond 6 o'clock.

JB: Unh huh

KINDNESS TO STRANGERS

ES: Yeah. And another thing too I remember about growing up with him is that he had this sense of compassion that we always used to be amazed because we know many times people would come, complete strangers and they would say, "Mr. Sprauve we have no place to sleep." And he would say "Come on." And we would have to go and find someplace for them to sleep, but he would accommodate them, not having the least idea who they are....I remember his firmness, about that book of Proverbs every time we did something wrong you had to get a lecture from Proverbs.

[Both laugh].

JB: But you know even when he was entertaining the strangers, so to speak, in the Bible it speaks about being kind to strangers because you might entertain angels unawares.

ES: Oh, yes, yes, yes, yes, yes!

JB: So probably, you know …

ES: I remember one time he got angry with my brother Verne and me. A gentleman came and we did not know who the gentleman was and he asked Mr. Sprauve if he could sleep there. My father said yes. And it was late at night. My father asked my brother and me to assemble this mahogany bed, one of these big four poster mahogany beds, so the gentleman could sleep on it. But we didn't know anything about assembling the bed, so we got the bed up somehow and as the man went on the bed, the bed came crashing down with him. And our father said we did it willfully because he felt we didn't want the man to stay there. But we didn't do it willfully. [laughs]

NEW-FANGLED APPLIANCE

I find that he was so set in some of the old ways. Change did not come quickly for him, especially with modern things. I remember one time somebody brought a gas stove in the house. And the stove was not hooked up at all. And he said "Get that thing out of here before it explode in the house, burn down the house!" [laughs] And we tried to tell him, no, no, no, no, it is not hooked up. He said, "Get it out of here! I don't want it."

DAILY MENU

And as a St. Johnian, he had to have fish every day. And if he didn't eat fish every day he was being starved, he couldn't find food. He had to have fish every day.

HOW NOT TO BE A BUSINESSMAN

ES: And something too, I remember that sometimes if somebody sent a list to him for groceries, let's say the person may have wanted 10 lbs. of flour and he happened to be out of flour that day. He would send us to St. Thomas to buy the 10 lbs. of flour for the person and then charge them with no interest that there was money paid for transportation and what not. He would just charge them the price that he normally would charge them even if he may have paid more to buy the flour. If he had a lower price, he would still charge them the lower price. [laughs]

JB: I guess it was a combination of business and welfare.

ES: Many times too, people would come in there and again we have seen complete strangers come here and he didn't know who they were and they wanted to get groceries, they had no money and he would say, "Oh yeah, tell them ... they could have the groceries." and of course many of them he never saw again.

ES: I remember then too his having the grocery store in Coral Bay.

JB: Yes. I shopped there many a day.

ES: I remember him riding the horse back and forth between here and Coral Bay. Sometimes he would be

Page from account book of Julius Sprauve. 1936 prices of basic commodities.

Loaned by Elroy Sprauve

down here in Cruz Bay, sometimes he would be in Coral Bay.

I remember the sailboats he had that he used to bring the groceries for the store. Sometimes the sailboat would stop in here, drop off some of the stuff and then take the rest to Coral Bay.

He enjoyed the grocery store, but deep down I don't think he was a businessman.

JB: I was thinking while you were talking about him that in those days it would have been rare, I think for a businessman to have businesses in both Coral Bay and Cruz Bay.

ES: Yes, yes. He did not have that genius, I think, of making a profit. I think to him his business became almost like a social agency. I remember people coming, his friends coming. If he did any campaigning that's where it was done because people would come to shop and it would be something like a 6 or 8 hour visit. They would shop and then he would feed them and they would talk and talk and talk.

JB: They would eat food from the store?

ES: Yes, he would have like when my mother prepared food and then he would serve them. But I don't think his sense of business as far as making a profit … I don't think he was a shrewd businessman at all. I must say he did something right with the St. John customers because they were so loyal to him. I know many persons wouldn't go shopping elsewhere as long as he had the grocery store there. They were sure to come there even if they bought things they might not need, but they had to patronize him.

JB: I remember my grandmother sending me with one of those black and white copybooks, and she would write her list down and one item I remember is "saltfish, no tail". My Aunt Pauline Thomas said she also wrote "cornmeal, no worms".

ES: [laughs]

JB: So maybe he did cater to his customers

ES: Yes! Yes!

JB: I don't remember him ever saying well, she shouldn't be specifying what part of the fish she wants.

HOW TO BE A POLITICIAN

ES: Those are most of the memories I have of him ... not so much as a politician. And again too, I don't think he was a politician in the truest sense of the way we think of politicians today. I think his thing was, of course in those days things were different. There was a need, some of the needs were obvious and the thing was to try to go and fulfill those needs. But as far as being crafty or knowing ways to get over, to get a vote, I don't think in those days it was very necessary because people in St. John tended to be very loyal to people whom they trusted.

JB: Now we'll talk about an organization with which he was associated.

THE ST. JOHN BENEVOLENT SOCIETY

ES: Yeah, I know that I heard that there was a St. John Benevolent Society and my father had a piece of property in Pastory and there was a house there and that house later was also used for the first kindergarten for St. John, but I know it was also the headquarters for ... the St. John Benevolent Society where they collected money and helped persons who were in need, indigent persons on the island or somebody who had some emergency and they needed help. For many years I know that was the headquarters and he was involved in that Society.

JB: We don't have too many efforts of that kind nowadays, even though we do have people in need, where we have community-based organizations that assist people. We have more formal ones like the Red Cross and United Way and so forth, but real grass-roots organizations we don't have

ES: that many of.

Entrance to Julius E. Sprauve School, Cruz Bay, St. John

Photo: Cristina Kessler

JULIUS E. SPRAUVE SCHOOL

JB: No. You might want to mention something about Sprauve School and how it came to be named after him.

ES: You know that he worked hard to get Estate Enighed and Contant for homestead purposes, for people to build homes and the area where the school is now was a ballfield, which I think that was part of the homestead project, that land, and I think because it was rather flat he got a part for them to hold on to for government purposes. So that when it came time for them to build the school that property had already belonged to the government. And I think he also worked hard on getting the funding for the school. I think that's why it was named for him.

THE HOMESTEAD PROGRAM

JB: I know a lot of people benefited, a lot of St. Johnians and people even from St. Thomas, a few of them benefited from the homestead program. I don't remember the exact amount of some of the lots.

ES: I think the average price was $19 for a house plot or some persons were able to get 5-acre tracts of land for $125, individual home plots for around $19. And that encompassed all the area bordering where the Westin is now all the way to the Cruz Bay Cemetery.

FOSTER CHILDREN

JB: You mentioned that he had two foster children, I believe you could almost call them foster children?

ES: Yeah, foster children because I mean there was not much of a welfare agency, but on the one estate that he had named Glucksberg, there was a lady who was living there and she had twin boys, Iva and Isaac. She was very dear, but apparently she died and these two boys were left alone and my father kind of adopted them and raised them till they became adults. They weren't any blood relatives of his, but I guess they had nowhere to go so he raised them.

INSTITUTIONALIZED CARE FOR YOUTH

JB: And St. John still has no place for homeless young people. No institution or anything like that for them.

ES: But you know this, I think sometime maybe a presentation should be made about this whole institution of godparents. Godparents came to the rescue for so many children.

JB: And raised their godchildren. So at one time there really was no need for a public institution. Well, in later days, though we had the Baptist Camp.

ES: But before that, you know, even the Queen Louise Home for children, some people from St. John went there.

JB: To St. Thomas?

ES: To St. Croix

JB: And then we had the schools at Leinster Bay and Calabash Boom.

ES: I know a lady now, she was here in St. John some time ago. Her maiden name was Smalls, but when her mother died she went to the Queen Louise Home in St. Croix.

JB: I never really thought about it, but even now I don't think that there is … Is there a home in St. Thomas for children? Or are all of them in St. Croix?

ES: I don't know of any home in St. Thomas. As far as I know they are all in St. Croix.

JB: So maybe they still have children in St. Thomas who end up in Queen Louise.

THE ROWBOAT COMMUTE

You might want to mention something about the way your father got to work when he was in the Legislature because of course he had to commute from St. John to St. Thomas and in those days we didn't have ferries that ran every hour.

ES: Yeah, I know he had sailboats. And he never sailed himself, but he had people who captained the boats. And I remember distinctly he had a big rowing boat by the name of the Blue Bell. And I can still see him sitting in the back and these two men rowing him to St. Thomas. I can't get that image out of my mind, what it must have been for these two men to row all the way to St. Thomas.

JB: I hope that it was smooth. Or at least not too rough.

ES: I would think maybe they, they must have tuned in to the weather and currents and maybe chose time to go when it was relatively calm.

HOMEBODY

JB: And you did say he liked to come home every

ES: Yeah, he hated the idea of having to sleep any night away from St. John. It had to be where he had to do it. He never voluntarily slept a night away from St. John.

JB: Did he travel much off island like to the States or Puerto Rico?

ES: No, I think he

JB: In the course of his work he didn't have to?

ES: No he didn't have to. I don't think he ever in his life went to the United States.

I know he had gone to Puerto Rico and one time late in his life he went to Nevis to the sulphur springs to see if it would help with his arthritis. But I've never known him to take any trip to the U.S. mainland.

A PLASTER FOR EVERY SORE

JB: You mentioned that he quoted Proverbs quite a bit And maybe you could mention one or two?

ES: Yes, from the Book of Proverbs in the Bible, the one that he used to mention a great deal was:

"Obedience is Heaven's first law." I remember hearing that one many times and getting a lecture on that. And I remember one time I was saying that when one of my brothers was in a fight, and he heard about it, he said "If your bed can't hold you, the earth will hold you!" But he always had a lot of sayings, he used a lot of sayings. I remember he always had some proverb for every occasion. And he was an avid reader. He read every little book, everything he came across with writing he would read. He read everything he could get his bands on. He would read and read.

HOW NOT TO HAVE GOOD HEALTH

But another thing too, he did not believe in going to doctors. I don't recall him ever going to see a doctor.

JB: He probably used a lot of home rememdies.

ES: He suffered terribly from arthritis. But he would never go to see a doctor.

Julius Sprauve holds the double honor of being the first St. Johnian elected to the Municipal Council of the Virgin Islands in 1936 and to the First Legislature of the Virgin Islands in 1954. With this latter election, he became the first Senator from the island of St. John.

In documenting his grandfather's life, Dr. Wilbur A. Sprauve wrote: "Whenever necessary, he would use his large row boat the Blue Bell to get to St. Thomas, getting Mr. Matthew Stevens or Mr. Josephus Williams to row him over, and though it would take hours (by boat and by foot) to get to the Legislative Chambers, he maintained a perfect attendance record."

Some of his achievements include advocating for and succeeding in obtaining property in the Enighed and Contant estates to be sold for homeownership, getting a new school, expanding and developing roads, and increasing health services, welfare services and water storage.

Senator Sprauve was never defeated in his campaigns and gave his home island twenty years of dedicated and productive service.

Joshua Ezekiel Stevens

December 31, 1899 – August 29, 1971

By Louisa Stevens Duzant and Mathilda Stevens Harvey

Joshua Stevens,
on the right.

CHURCH ACTIVITY

My father, Joshua Ezekiel Stevens, was an ordained Deacon in Emmaus Moravian Church and he ministered the gospel of Jesus to the people.

I was very young when he was ministering, but after he died my sister gave me his books of sermons and they are awesome! I couldn't believe it! But, yes I could, because I'm in the ministry myself. So when I read them it assured me that he was truly a man of God. And as he always said, "As for me and my house, we will serve the Lord." You see he was truly a Joshua.

He sang tenor in the choir and loved to sing. He and my mother both sang in the choir. And we as children had to sing also. But, he led by example. It wasn't until I went to New York and joined the church a few years after that I met a young man that sang just like my father, that nasal tenor.

FAMILY MAN

He had three children with my mom, Mary: my brother Godwin who is the oldest, my sister, Mathilda the youngest and me. And he always thought that we were enough company for each other. So we didn't get to mingle too much with the other kids, except for church and school. At home we had to play with each other. But it was fun growing up in that household because we knew we were loved by our parents.

He was a wonderful husband to my mother. And I found myself always looking for a man with his qualities, one that I haven't found as yet. Ha! Ha! Ha! Ha! But he loved my mother like Christ loved the church. He was a godly man. And he loved his children. And *he was the head of his household.* And what Papa say, went.

POLICE OFFICER

He was also a policeman. If I remember correctly, he joined the Police Force when there were Constables. They weren't called "policemen" as yet. I believe it was the year I was born, but it was months before I was born in 1942, that he was the first police officer in Coral Bay. The first. And, you know, he went to all the classes. I also have some of his notes from those classes. He believed in advancing himself.

I remember when a hurricane was coming how my father had to go and put up the hurricane warning. He had the different flags that tell you how serious the hurricane was going to be, you know. And then he would board up our house and different members of the family would come and stay at our house and the adults would be praying and we would be in a corner playing. But those were the good old days.

I remember he had his office in the Police Station which you can say was a room in the Coral Bay Clinic. It was a building on the Benjamin Franklin School grounds that had a clinic, a classroom and his police room. He would go in there and listen to the radio at certain times of the day. He had to be in there because they would have broadcasts over the police radio as to what's going on and what's what.

My father was a friend to the young people. He talked to the young people who were doing mischief as though he were their father. He would lecture them. And he would chase them out the mango tree. And they would coop him and he would coop them. But they all respected him as the police officer.

It amazes me now that when my father was a police officer in Coral Bay and we were growing up there was no crime. Everybody used to keep their doors unlocked. Open. Yes, as I was saying, there was no crime and it was a pleasure to know you were going out and you leave your door open, you know nobody was going into your house. Here I am, 47 years later, I come home I got to lock up my door. You know, and

I hate to pick up the newspapers cause you read all this distressing stuff. But, it was a nice community. Everybody looked out for each other and took care of each other. Matter of fact, the village raised the children. 'Cause everybody looked out for the young people. And so they could have spanked us. You can't hit the kids now and you see what's going on today. You know, and they would tell your parents and then you'd get spanked again. Now parents don't want to hear nothing about the kids. But we need to go back to the old days—some of the old things that work. That's why I'm the woman I am today. You know when I was young I thought he was very strict. But I really appreciated it when I grew older. And I really thanked him for being the kind of dad that he was, concerned about us, disciplined, you know. And I got to tell him how much I appreciated it when he came to New York. As we grew older and I had my kids, I found myself doing the same thing he did, you know, with my children. And I thank God for that.

When he first started doing police work his vehicle was a horse. As the island progressed, then his mode of transportation was the jeep. He used to drive a jeep around Coral Bay and backwards and forwards to Cruz Bay when it was necessary.

BUSINESSMAN

My father also was a businessman. He had a jeep rental. He had the first jeep rental in Coral Bay. He was the first of a lot of things.

FARMER

My father also was a gardener. He loved to plant. He had three "grounds" [gardens]: one Bordeaux Road, one Johnny Hone, and one down below the house. Sometimes we used to go with him and make it a picnic outing when it was time to harvest the sweet potatoes, the tannia, cassava, the eddoes—the eddoe bush for kallaloo. The one at the house had okra, black eyed peas, eggplants, and the stuff you use regularly. But the yam, sweet potatoes, tannia, etc. that was Bordeaux Hill. On Johnny Hone he had the mangoes. We also had a lot of cane down by our house and Johnny Hone. And we used to have a cane party. Cause he'd come back with a cane and we'd sit down and he'd peel the cane and we'd eat the cane. It was wonderful! It was a wonderful life growing up here on the island.

We also raised chickens so we had fresh eggs and chickens. We didn't eat meat every day. But we had meat on Sundays for sure. Sometimes we would eat one of the chickens. During the week we had soup, saltfish, things like that. At that time people didn't eat a whole lot of meat.

Then we had goats and pigs. My father was an all-around farmer, gardener, fisherman, you name it. And he was generous 'cause he used to share what he had with the neighbors. When he harvested his garden he would send some potatoes for Mama Lou, or Auntie Consuelo, Auntie Esther, Miss Viola— the people around. Same thing when he catched the fish—strap for this one, strap for that one. When he killed a goat—he had a piece for this one, a piece for that one. If he killed a pig, I remember Mama Lou liked to make blood pudding and so he used to save the blood from the pig for her to make the pudding. It was just wonderful because we had a great community life along with a wonderful family life.

FISHERMAN

My father was also a fisherman. He used to go to fish every day. He set his fishpots and my brother, Godwin, would go with him. Every day he'd go to pull his fishpots and take the fish out, so we had fish for breakfast, fish for lunch, fish for dinner.

My mother was a baker. When she had the oven on —she baked out of a brick oven—we would put the fish in hot ashes to roast and then put them in lime and salt water afterwards. That was the best fish, BEST, [laughs] and then we would have fried fish, stewed fish, you know, all kinds of fish.

BAKER

My mother used to bake and Papa helped her with like kneading of the bread or stirring of the sweetbread and putting them in the oven after they raised. So he used to watch my mom, you know my mom was the number one baker on the island at that time [laughs]. She used to make the sweetbread for the Lovefeast as well as for the Communion at church every first Sunday. So he used to watch her. And I was amazed when my mother died that he knew how to make the sweetbread. And he continued to make the sweetbread for the church and bake bread.

You know at that time we used to have a Lovefeast with bread and water before we had the wine and wafer. And you know, his baked goods were tasty! Not quite as good as mom, but they were good [laughs]. The only thing, I don't think he was a cook. He wasn't into real cooking. But he was a baker.

VISIT TO NEW YORK

He came to visit me in New York in 19 hundred and 68 about a week after my daughter was born. And he spent three months with us. He loved it, but he forgot that New York is a big town and was not like St. John where everybody knew him. My father would go to the corner and talk to the men, he would hold a conversation with them. He knew where the store was. I would send him for one thing and he would come back hours later and have a big story to tell me—who he met, who he was talking to, etc. But we had a good visit. And he got to see New York.

While he was visiting in New York, my cousin got married and I could not go to the wedding because I just had my daughter. So my husband took him and they both went to this wedding in the Bronx. I'm home in the bed with my daughter and my husband rings the doorbell in the night and I hollered out the window, "Who is it?" And he says "It's me!" And he was by himself. So I said "Where is my father?" He said, "He's not here?" I said, "No, he's not here and you better go and find him!" [laughs] He said, "Where am I supposed to ..." And I said, "I don't care where you find him, just go find him and bring him home.!" So my husband went to the corner. He looked east, he looked west, he looked north, he looked south. And then all of a sudden here comes Papa just humming. And my husband said, "Where you bin?" He said "Oh, I overshot the house, you know, and I went up the street and I met these young fellows [Something you don't do in New York] and I asked them where's the address?" And they pointed him how to get back and he came back. I was trying to tell my father, "You don't do that. You don't know who they are. And they know you're a stranger. All he could refer to was "You forgot I used to be a police officer? [laughs] He felt that he could take them on. I said "O.K. I thanked God that he was safe and he found his way back home. And guess what? You know the next day when my husband was talking about the wedding, he let me to know that Papa was the belle of the ball. Ha, Ha, he was dancing with everybody, you know, he was having a good time. That's the kind of person he was.

And I must say another little story. In the day-time when I felt better, I was going to visit a friend of mine with my daughter. I had my daughter in my arms and my father and I went to visit my friend. And we passed these young guys who said "Un huh, look at that old man with that young girl and the baby." I said "Papa, they think this baby is yours, they don't know you're my father." He said "What!" I said "Yeah, but we know different, so don't worry about it." [She laughs.]

THE GOOD OLD DAYS

In our community, when I was growing up, we used to have secular concerts in the school and spiritual ones in the church. We had quadrille dancing and my mother and my father were good partners with each other. And there were plays—live plays—to me they were better than Broadway sometimes, most times. That's how we entertained ourselves. We, the young ones, got to do skits and say recitations—and not with paper. We had to remember it all. And we'd sing the hillbilly songs, etc. We sang hymns and Sankeys, the church songs. One of the main activities of the year was the Sunday School picnic when the church came together. My mom cooked the food and my father took it to church and all that stuff. On Easter Monday when we had the picnic we used to have the Cricket Match. We had horse races. Easter Monday was the big day. The horse races used to be down Carolina, nowadays, the level stretch of the King's Hill Road, up that road, Carolina Flat. And the Cricket Match used to be on the Flat, the Emmaus Ballfield, aka the Coral Bay Ballfield. And I just loved to see the men who played cricket in their white uniforms, I mean lily, sparkling white outfits, and my father would be patrolling and working and entertaining sometimes at the same time. You know, but those were the good old days. And then we would have dances at the school—Benjamin Franklin School, now the Guy H. Benjamin School, where they would play these old-time two steps and the quadrille and the square dances, the things that the young people don't know how to dance these days. All they know to do is you know what, the calypso. But you know, I liked to look at them dancing—the old folks doing those dances so gracefully.

"Friend Joshie" was one way that Patrolman Joshua Stevens was addressed. [In his day if you were not a relative or godparent with the proper designations: "Auntie," etc. you were a "friend."]

He kept excellent order in Coral Bay during the days when policemen wore guns more for decoration than function. That was, except for the time that he kept warning one of the ladies in Emmaus Village to keep her hog, a public nuisance, in her yard. One day as he was going to work he encountered the hog creating mayhem as usual on the Emmaus Church grounds. The students at the Benjamin Franklin School, who saw him and the hog, stopped their activities and anticipated his next action. A well-placed bullet got rid of the problem once and for all. He then went and told the lady to retrieve her property.

Committed to his work, he did not stop when the sun went down. At night he was known to have chased boys out of mango trees between the graveyard and the church.

As a lay preacher and Sunday School teacher, he was actively engaged in church life. He also sang in the secular concerts that were held on the first floor of the Emmaus Manse. A song that he sang was "Catch a Falling Star" by Perry Como (1957). One of his former Sunday School students remembers that he paid him as well as his father when they both worked on his house unlike some other men for whom they were employed.

Austin Walters
August 2, 1922 – June 28, 2006

Austin Walters,
Photo: Oswin Sewer, Sr.

Interview of Austin Walters at his home in Lindberg Bay, St. Thomas, 1990.

BEYOND DOUBLOON HILL

One Saturday, Eddie Moorehead, Neptune Richards, and myself decided let's go for a ride. And they said, "Where you going Stino?" So well, "Let's go for a ride up the hill." Started up the hill, they still insist to me, "Where you going?" I say, "Let's go for a ride." So we got up as far as where at first you only could go with the truck and no! you only could go there with an animal. You couldn't go there with no vehicle at all, because there was no vehicle. And when we got there with this jeep, Mr. Richards, Neptune, asked me, "Where you goin, Stino?" I say, well, I want to try something. He say, "Way you goin, not down that hill?" I say, "Yes, I'm going down that same hill." He say, "Man, you gonna kill us." I say, "No. Anyhow how we go, we'll go together—three friends." So we started down the hill and at the bottom of the hill there was a road we called Old Works. When I got there, I realized what I have to do next, so I turned the jeep around. I managed to turn the jeep around, get back up the hill and back to Cruz Bay. Told everybody how far we been with the jeep and they said uhh, everybody thought it was crazy. Everybody say, 'uhh Stino, man, you crazy, Walters you crazy, Walters you crazy." That's all right.

FROM CRUZ BAY TO CORAL BAY BY JEEP

1st Trip

Then the Thursday of the following week, Austin Smith, my good friend, and I decided to come to St. Thomas to have a little fun. Come down here, we had a couple of beers, then we went home the evening. I went to work. Round 11 o'clock that night, Austin Smith came to me. He said "Wha you doin?" I say, "Nothing. Just waiting for time to knock off." Meantime I had the jeep outside the building. Full of gas and everything. I said to him, I said, "Stino, let's go Coral Bay." He say, "Yo really goin?" I said "Yes. You'll go with me?" He say, "Sure man. Let's go." So with 12 o'clock I snapped the lock on the door, shut off everything, and we started for Coral Bay.

All right. We started for Coral Bay. When we got on top the hill where we call Doubloon [pronounced "Dublin"] Hill I stopped. We removed the spare tire of the jeep, put it inside the jeep because at that time, the spare tire was carried on the side of the jeep. So he said, "Stino, yo tink we could make it?" Ah say, "Yes man, we make it man." And we started down the hill quite slowly and nice. And we get to Old Works. He say, "How we goin round?" Ah say, "Ah done see it." Turn up, we went around the hill, round the ruins and started going up this particular area was like steps, so the jeep was like going up steps all the way because it was pure rocks. Even horses and donkeys have to take it very slowly going up and down that area. Then when we got up to the area they call Bordeaux Gap, he say "How you turn this thing around this place?" He say, "Stino, man, how you'n do it? We can't turn back, we can't back down [reverse]." I say "We goin' aroun."

And ah maneuver the jeep, maneuver the jeep, until he say, "Stino yo make it!" Ah say "Yes", and we started up over the hill that at that time was called Mamey Garden.

Then we got over the hill, get up on the top of the hill, and we looked down and could see Coral Bay down in the distance. And we continued traveling, continued traveling, and then we get to another area we call King's Hill. We start going down the hill, there was one particular area we had to take down a portion of the fence, that it had like a gate, we moved the one post so that the jeep could get through and went down the hill, got down the hill, he say, "Man that's death. You can't turn that area there we gon' kill ourselves." I say, "No, I'm going show you, teach you something tonight."

And we went down that particular area and we turned it and we went down the hill to get down to Carolina level. When we got in Carolina level, he start to sing and jump up. Then the windshield of the jeep, I didn't have it strapped down, and it came up and almost crushed one of his fingers. So, I took him to the nurse, Mrs. Nathaniel, that was the nurse at the time over at Calabash Boom. And she took care of the finger. It wasn't crushed, it was like squeezed a little and she took care of the finger. Then we left Calabash Boom, which she wanted to know how we traveled to Calabash Boom, how we got there. And I told her the same place the horse and donkeys traveled, we traveled with the jeep. Then we went back to Coral Bay and we stopped to his brother"

JB: Fred

AW: Fred Smith. So then the party began because all the fellows that we knew came around because they saw the lights coming over the hill, they heard the sound, and everybody come like a party that night. And the next morning we left pretty early, get back to Cruz Bay, because the patrolman at the time was Mr. Stevens

JB: Mr. Joshua Stevens

AW: Joshua Stevens. He had called the Administrator, which was Mr. George Simmonds, and tell him what had happened the night. So when I got in Cruz Bay, I met with him. He asked me if I was crazy. I said, "No, sir." He say, "Where you passed with the jeep?" I say, "I'll show you one of these days." He say, "Not me!" And then it rest at that.

FROM CRUZ BAY TO CORAL BAY BY JEEP

2nd Trip

The following Monday, Mr. Simmonds called me and when I got down on the dock I saw Governor

DeCastro, I saw Mr. Boreham, saw Dante De Lagarde. I say "Mornin Chief." I say "What's wrong? I thought something was wrong, you had come to chat with me or something." He say, "No." He say, "Mister, 'tis you is the crazy man?" That's what the Governor ask me. I say, "No, Governor, what make you think so?" He say "Well, you going to show me way you pass with the jeep, cause it's only crazy people does do these things in the night." I say, "Well, let's go."

JB: Now, Mr. Boreham at that time was

AW: Commissioner of Public Works

JB: Commissioner of Public Works, and who was Mr. De Lagarde?

AW: He was the Assistant.

JB: And then you had the Administrator

AW: of St. John

JB: George Simmonds. So it was 5 of you.

AW: Yes, the Governor, The Commissioner of Public Works, his Assistant Commissioner, The Administrator of St. John and myself. So we got in this jeep. I must first tell you that by that time the government had got a jeep ….so we took that jeep and um, we started up the hill. When we got to Doubloon Hill again, I said to the party, I said "Well, gentlemen, this is it. After now there's no turning back." So the Governor asked me "How you mean there's no way you can turn the jeep back?" I said, "No sir. After now there's no turning back. Straight to Coral Bay." He say, "O.K., let's go." When we got to Bordeaux Gap they asked, "How you going to turn this round here? Explain me." I say, "I'll show you." And I turned it round there. They say, "Oh my God, I never see anything like this before!" Then we went up over Mamey Garden, up over the other hills quite comfortable, then when we got down to King's Hill that was the place that they all got scared because we were facing the drop bout 200 feet down! And ah, they all want to know well what would happen if the jeep slipped or got away. I say well, you can't think on that. And we went round, went round. The Governor looked back. He say, "I came from up there?" "Yes sir. We certainly did."

JB: And then Mr. Boreham, when you were about to go down was when he wanted to sit behind you?

AW: That's right. He wanted to sit behind me as to keep balance the jeep, as he said, because he was heavier than I were and he was sitting on the bad side, so he wanted to sit behind me, which was the solid side to keep the jeep down on that side. So he changed and we went down.

AND when we got down in Coral Bay, we went over to the Marsh's place. They greet the Governor and everybody else and were so happy to see us. Then we went over to Mr. Fred Smith place and they all had a drink there, coke and thing like that, and when we was ready to go back, I ask him if he was ready to go back. The Governor say, "No, we'n going back with you. You going back alone." I say, "What you mean?" I say, "Wha you afraid of?" He say, "No, I am going back on the Coast Guard boat." So I remained there with them until the Coast Guard boat came. They get on the boat and we turned off. And I get back in Cruz Bay before the boat.

JB: So they had to call Cruz Bay for the boat.

AW: Yeah

JB: And in those days there were no telephones in Coral Bay.

AW: Radio communications. Mr. Stevens was the operator and policeman at the time. So he called to Cruz Bay and it was the twelve o'clock time when they used to call St. Thomas or Cruz Bay. People wanted to know where I passed, but I was customed to go there. And then after that Mr. Simmonds got Mr. Boreham to okay to widen the various parts that was difficult for the jeep to go round in one turn. So then they widened the place and then it was able to go round with the jeep in one turn ordinary and then transportation started from Coral Bay to Cruz Bay.

THE NEW TRUCK

AW: Then shortly after that, must have been 6 months after to a year, the old truck that they had

JB:　The government truck

AW: Government truck, yes turned over. It slipped from where we were carrying sand and I asked Mr. Julius Sprauve, Councilman for St. John, for a new truck to replace the old CCC camp truck. He told me some new trucks were coming in and if it got mashed up he would get a new one. I backed the Camp truck up a hill by the reservoir, ran it on a high stone which tilted the truck and jumped out. The truck fell down on the catchment of the reservoir and that was the end of it. And uh, after that Mr. Sprauve insist for Mr. Boreham to send him a new truck. And he did send him a new truck. About a week later, it came up on the barge. Then one of the boys, Herman Sprauve, I teach to run the truck, to operate the truck, another one, named ….Herbert Sprauve. He, too, learned to drive the truck. So when the new truck came they started to um work, drive the truck, I stopped. And you couldn't get this new truck go up the hill. They used to take the mall, dig the mall, right where the school is.

JB:　Uh hunh, Julius Sprauve School.

AW: Yes. Take the mall from there to care [carry] on the road, to repair the road. But this new truck couldn't get up the hill. I remember Mr. Leander Francis came up, he and another mechanic from Public Works. They came up and they checked and they did everything that was feasible possible but they still couldn't get the truck to go up the hill.

So one night I was sitting in the power station and I had the truck up there, cause I used to park it up there, and a thought came to me, and I said, um, I'm going to take a chance. I took the carburetor off of the truck, and under the carburetor they have never checked that area, there was a governor that controlled the speed of the truck. So I took it off, put back the carburetor, went down the hill, the street, with the truck, turned around, and went right up over the hill. As easy as anything could be with the truck. The next morning, I went where they had the mall, and get Christian, that's the old guy, to load the truck with mall. Men was on the road working, digging mall from the side of the hill to patch the road. And I drove the truck that day right up with the load of mall. When they saw the truck they say, "How, What happen? What happen? How the truck came up the hill? How you get it work?" It's all right.

JB: Heh, heh. You didn't tell anybody?

AW: No. And I had this piece of metal in a tool pan for years, years. It was when I was leaving the Knud Hansen Hospital it came out the pan then. It was in that pan for years, for over 20 years. And they never knew. I never told them what had happened. And the truck, rrrrr up the hill as easy as ever. You see, this governor was a flat piece of metal they had, with just a little tiny hole in the center and sufficient gas wasn't going through this hole to give the power for the truck. So after I removed it she got everything. Oh, man, this truck would have almost go up the hill in high speed!

JB: Mmm, hmm

AW: Yeah, I been all over St. John with that jeep.

JB: After you went to Coral Bay, then you decided to do a bit more exploring

AW: Johns Folly, all down on the north side

JB: You went up Johnny Hone, the road by Emmaus Church and went over the hill to Leinster Bay?

AW: Right down. As long as there was space for a donkey to travel, I traveled with the jeep in St. John.

JB: Did you go to East End?

AW: I didn't go to East End. That's the only place I didn't go, to East End. But all over the place I've been, up as far past Harry Samuel…Rehoboth, Palestina up on top the hill there, I didn't go down. But that's the only place I didn't go to is East End. But all other place I've been to on St. John. All where the Gibneys, Hawks Nest and all those places. Before you turn down to go down King's Hill there's a road to go down to Marsh's place down on the north, Maho Bay! I've been all from the King's Hill Road right round Maho Bay come right back to Cruz Bay.

JB: Anh, ha. And these roads were more like donkey tracks.

AW: Donkey tracks, exactly. Then they put bulldozer on them. As fast as I go through a place and they find out where I've been, they put

JB: Then they put a bulldozer because they figure that

AW: yes, yes

JB: they could make it.

THE ART OF DRIVING

AW: You know where Little Cinnamon? All right. Corey Bishop has a place up there or had a place up there, right beyond Gerhardt Sprauve place. There's a road go up right there, and could come right down to Little Cinnamon and come back to Cruz Bay. All there I've been. I took paths with bulldozer and big tracks. I had to drive the jeep from the side, outside the jeep. I put it in gear with the bulldozer track on the jeep, the men walking behind. And I put my clutch in, put it in low gear and everything and let's go and drive the jeep from the outside, walking outside the jeep to come from down there. The bulldozer just cut the road and it was muddy, it was slippery, so and we wanted to get the track out so we could repair it. The only way to get it out was to put it on the jeep. We get it on the jeep and there was no room for me to sit. It was when we got up on the hill we got block and tackle, raised it up, and put it in the truck to bring it back to Cruz Bay. But no truck couldn't go down there where it was, where the bulldozer had stopped.

JB: So you had a jeep driving without a driver. Steering from outside. That must have been going very slow.

AW: Yeah, very slow, very slow. Low low 4-wheel drive, very low. We raised the adjustment in the carburetor just a little so that it doesn't stall, but she kept going rrrrrrrr and we walked it sideways straight up the hill cause she was pulling herself and she was also pulling us. So it was no problem, you know.

JB: Yeah.

AW: So, I know the jeep. I could tell you about the jeep.

JB: What I liked was when you were going down, you had mentioned to me a little bit earlier about when you were going down King's Hill and you had to give it a little gas and a little clutch

AW: That's right.

JB: to get around that

AW: that curve, yes

JB: hairpin, that bad corner there.

AW: You see how it was at that time, you couldn't neutralize altogether and put in gear and depend on releasing your clutch to come back. What I did was I partially neutralized the machine. She was in gear, yet she was in neutral. It's what we drivers would call "riding the clutch." In other words, a percentage forward she neutralize, a percentage backward she in gear. You see, so your foot would be on the acceleration all times and one way would neutralize her and one way would energize her. So when you want to go to neutralize her, just let her go, press in her clutch she go forward a little, let it back, she come back, you don't have to be switching foot. In other words, at that particular time you didn't use your brakes, just the accelerator and the clutch.

That's how I brought the cement up when I was building this house —his home in Lindberg Bay, St. Thomas—to cast the floor. The man came and he say he wasn't coming up there. I asked him if he would let me use the truck, bring the truck up. If anything happen to the truck, I'll pay you for the truck and the materials. He say, "You've ever driven a truck yet?" I say "Probably before you born." And I brought the concrete truck up here

JB: up this hill

AW: before this was paved and that road was the worst place in the world. Right there. And she came up. She wouldn't turn the curve in no first, so I had to do the same thing. She went back and after that? Putting all, she was a 10-wheeler, putting all the load there was, and there was nothing to stop her from coming. But it was first get around the corner.

DEENIE & CHAMP

JB: Now, I like the story that you told about the lady in Cruz Bay, Miss Adina Prince?

AW: Adina Prince.

JB: Aha, and her boxer dog. Could you tell us that story?

AW: Well, heh, heh, Champ. Yeah, Champ was a boxer. Lovely dog, nice dog, devoted dog. And he used to be along every day with Adina Prince, her name were. And then in the evening he'll come to me, to stay with me. And this day, we had missed Deenie for a couple of hours. She didn't come home at her usual time, so everybody get, you know, kind of upset, wonder where she were, and if anything had happened to her. But then they saw the dog, you know, so then they came to me, they came to me and they asked me about Deenie. If Deenie had come, where she is? If I'n see her? I say, "No." I say "Well, the dog here. Something must be wrong. Follow the dog." And they went back with the dog. I think the time when the dog had went and find Deenie when she had fall down round the rock? Yeah, and he went

JB: So anyway,

AW: They found her and they brought her home.

JB: Unh, huh.

AW: And the next incident we had with that dog, Aunt Deenie, was the night when she wanted to prove to me that she was the master of that dog.

JB: This was because the dog used to spend

AW: the day with her and the night with me. And she wanted to prove that the dog was her dog, because she had all prerogative. She used to have him all day long. Wherever she traveled, she traveled with that dog. You couldn't touch her, he'd look to bite you.

JB: Ohh

AW: Yeah, you couldn't touch her. You couldn't touch Deenie at all. He'd look to bite you or thing like that, so he was like her bodyguard. So she felt that, that was it! But then, after night, his duty end at that certain time and it begins at a certain time. So this night when I told her what to do, she came up to the Power Station, and she didn't call him and she start coming towards me and I sic him on her and he jumped her. I called him back. Then I sic him on her again. He did the same thing. The third time, she say, "Champ? That's wha you doin to me? You would look to bite Deenie?" Then he stopped, he looked at her, he walked around her and smelled her to make sure it was Deenie and then his little nubby tail started shaking. He recognize her then and everything, but he still, he still didn't follow her. He came and lie down side of me.

AW: I said, "Go Champ!" he wouldn't go then. He had recognize her and everything. But he knew that his duty was with me that time of the day.

FRIENDS

AW: I had a nice life in St. John. I had a lot of friends, especially the Smiths—Austin Smith, Fred Smith, Lillian, Alma, then Herman came, especially the old man, their father, Charles Smith. Charles Smith took me to St. John, me and my whole household. The

Lillian was his boat.

Yeah! I had a good life in St. John. I was happy. Me and the administrator was very close. Very, very close. Like when we go Tortola for August Monday. The people in St. John were so nice that if they see the Government boat wasn't at the dock they know I'm on Tortola. And they don't fuss. They don't have light that night, they don't fuss. Because when I go up to work at night if I'm reading a book, sometime I read till one, two o'clock and they got power all the time.

JB: And you were the only operator

AW: for a certain time. for a certain time. Before I came down to work in St. Thomas again, I trained Robert O'Connor, Bob, to run the generator. And he used to run the generator. I first started to teach Tony Boynes. Then afterward. Tony used to work hard and he used to be tired, but Bob used to work over at Caneel Bay. I teach Bob to drive the truck too! He used to work at Caneel Bay and then he wanted to learn the operation of the generator, so I taught Bob. Bob and I was like brothers. After I moved to St. Thomas, I could of go to St. John and if there was any special occasion that I wanted to attend I used Bob clothes.

JB: That was being close.

AW: Yeah! Yeah, I remember when, um Harry Samuel died. I went to his funeral. I didn't know until I got there the day that Mr. Harry had died. And Harry was very close. And I say, "Bob, man, I so sorry that I can't go to the funeral." And he say, "What happen? Why you can' go?" I say, "Man I'n got no clothes." He say, "Man go in the house, put on may clothes, man." So I went in his place, take my bath and everything, put on his clothes—everything! Shoes, the only thing I didn't put on of his own was his shorts, his undergarments, but his shirt, tie, everything—well-dressed, blue serge suit, and I went to the funeral. Robert O'Connor and I was very close in St. John, very close, we were like brothers. Up to this day. If I go to St. John tomorrow as long as he see me he will give me a jeep to drive.

JB: Uh huh

AW: This is yours, Stino, you drive that.

JB: Yeah

AW: Yeah. Another young fellow that I was very close, you know, up to now—Myron.

JB: Callwood?

AW: He work to the, um,

JB: to the Park?

AW: Park. Tall guy? Oh man, he's like my son. It isn't a time that he see me that he don't hug me up. All them used to be round me. Teaching them mechanical work and everything. I used to repair machines for Caneel Bay, too. Those tractors, they had 14 tractors. They have sent them over there to me and I repaired them.

THE ART OF SAILING

AW: Then we had another guy came up there to be with Loredon Boynes. When Loredon started the fleet of jeeps that he had up there, Urman Fredericks, a little short guy, start to work with Loredon and he also became engineer for the government boat. You know Wilmot Blackwood? You had know Wilmot Blackwood?

JB: My uncle. My aunt's husband.

AW: Yes. Well, he was

JB: the boat captain?

AW: Yes an engineer for the boat. And then when Urman came, the two of them, you know because there was two boat at one time—the picket boat which was a Coast Guard type little boat and the big 50-footer that they had. So one used to run this, and they used to alternate. All before Boynes became captain of the boat. Well, they always wanted Boynes to work because Boynes, Loredon Boynes, is one of the best sea captains there is in St. John.

JB: Probably in the Virgin Islands?

AW: In Hip! Hip! Hurrah! I believe one of the best there is around these islands, Loredon Boynes. Loredon Boynes as I know today, I don't know if he have the eyesight or what, was the only person that I know could ah take a boat, sailing boat, through St. Thomas Lagoon—go in one part and come out the other part. Loredon Boynes! He knew the whole of St. Thomas Lagoon.

JB: You mean other people would get lost?

AW: Lost, right! There's a lot of cays in that place, you know. You should see that Lagoon! It got people go in there, they can't get their way out. And Loredon could ah sail a boat in there and bring her back out. Furthermore, when he went away, I could recall he went away, I think to Florida. I think he used to be with Dr. Knight. You know a doctor, a dentist

JB: Yes, that lived in St. John.

AW: Yes, he has his house right on the bayside going to Gallows Point?

JB: I remember.

AW: Well, he took him to Florida someplace and Loredon make his mark by sailing a boat up there in Florida in a race. He was working on the boat and he told the man the sails are wrong. And the man asked him if he know to handle it better and he say, Yes, and he changed things around, Bop! The man win the race! First time! Of course you know the old people dem of Loredon, the Sprauve, they was master sailors and thing. Take Charles Smith, he used to go from St. John to St. Croix. Alone!

JB: Oh, I didn't know. He was my grandfather.

AW: Alone! He had a boat named the Lillian.

JB: Yeah, after one of his daughters.

AW: In those days he used to bootleg. He was living down Mary's Point at the time. And he could leave, say he was going to fish. He would take a load of liquor and go to St. Croix. Drop off the load of liquor, come back home, he alone. He was a good, good sailor.

We went in a race one time. The Lillian and the same Jurgen's. You know outside of Cruz Bay there's a reef. Right outside the harbor. And he passed over the reef with his boat! When we get near the reef, he say, "The two of you! Go down! and listen good and go on her one side and put the ballast on the one side!" And we changed the ballast put it up on the side of the boat. We heard a loud sound, crook, crook, fainter, crook. Then she get back off the reef we don't hear the sound. When you get close to rocks you hear a tapping sound, clook, clook, clook. After you don't hear this sound you clear. Put back the ballast and everything. Used to be fun. Lots of fun.

In those days, 4th of July and holidays and they planned a sail, Oh Man, it was a holiday for Cruz Bay! Yeah, man, you see all kind of old rum and thing bringing. Ha! ha! ha! It used to be fun. I enjoyed living in St. John.

RETURN TO ST. THOMAS

AW: But then when the um, Knud Hansen Memorial Hospital was about to open up Jeppesen wanted some-body to work with him, who knew somewhat about diesel engines and things like that. And he asked the Governor for me to transfer. Even Mr. Boreham didn't care about it

JB: He liked you in St. John?

AW: Yeahhh. He said "I thought you were a fixed thing in St. John. I didn't expect you would ever come back home to work." I say, "well, No-ooo." He say, "Well I understand you got your young daughter to go to school" and bro, bro, bro, bro, bro. He say, "All right, all right." That's when Robert O'Connor got my job.

WHITE MALL

AW: The building across the road from the genera-tor, which part it got the gas station now, was built by

Corey Bishop. You know that building was built out of mall and cement. White mall and cement. More white mall than what sand it had. That ain't gon fall down now. Not that.

JB: It's a strong building.

AW: That ain't gon fall down now, sweetheart.

JB: Yeah.

AW: Wet mall is said to come as hard as concrete. Without cement in it.

JB: You said all where the Julius Sprauve School is used to be white mall?

AW: Yes. The pit, we used to call it.

JB: Now when I remember it, it was maran.

AW: Well, because they let it grow up. They stopped digging mall. But they used to have mall all along the place. And one man used to do it. He'd dig for weeks.

JB: You remember who that was?

AW: Christian. A lil deafy old fellow.

NO TRAFFIC JAMS

JB: Mmm. Yeah. Um, there was something that you had mentioned before, too about Mr. Sprauve when he had a truck, or maybe a jeep first?

AW: A jeep, yeah.

JB: That was when there were very few jeeps in St. John.

AW: That's right. That was about the 4th jeep or the 5th jeep. Then who had a jeep in St. John, too, who I used to use commonly, that was like mines, a man who has a fleet of jeeps in Water Island now, name was Tom Ford. He used to live down on the point right across from Gerhardt Sprauve house? Yes! Yeah, well a few people used to have some apartment buildings right there on the end, the corner before you go round, well there was Tom Ford, very very close friend of mine.

And, um he had a jeep. I used to repair the jeep and everything. And use it whenever I want to use it.

CRUZ BAY BACK IN THE DAY

JB: So what did Cruz Bay look like when you first got up there?

AW: When I first saw Cruz Bay, Ah say, "This is a quiet place." And it were quiet, very quiet. In those days, Cruz Bay was a place where you could go to relax. I have leave my home, other fellows have leave their place and go down and sit down on a bench in Cruz Bay. Next thing you know you fall asleep. And nobody disturb you. Not today! Number one you got an amount of cars to wake you up and hell knows what and uhh people aren't as they used to be.

I used to leave St. John the last week of December, just push in the door and come down here. Me and my wife on vacation. And go back February.

JB: over a month later

AW: and the door just shut in, just like that.

JB: and everything exactly how you left it

AW: Just like how I leave it. Just like how I leave it.

AW: Angela Thomas used to live with Miss Roach. Verne Sprauve with Nana, Nana Sprauve. Verne was Julius Sprauve's son and Nana was his mother, Julius Sprauve's wife. They pass by the place. If it raining they shub in the door or the window or whatever it is and that was that.

JB: Ya

AW: 'Tain today. Today, see ah got three dogs here. Ah got eight guns in the house.

JB: People feel a need to protect themselves.

SANITATION DEPARTMENT AND THE DUMP

JB: You had mentioned, Mr. Walters, that there was

a gentleman who used to take care of the sanitation in Cruz Bay. Perhaps you could tell us a little bit about Public Works and the Sanitation Department in those days when you first came to St. John.

AW: Yes, yes when I went to St. John in those days, there was a gentleman, an old gentleman by the name of Leopold Jacobs. He used to sweep the street every morning, go round, all day you could find him sweeping and taking up the garbage or the dirt with a wheelbarrow and putting it in a particular area to burn when there was a chance he could burn a little at a time. Wasn't burning too much, but just a little at a time.

Then after a time we got a truck from Mr. Boreham in Public Works that we started to clean the area, take up all the old debris, old whatever it was people could put out, we started to take it up and carry it to the dump which was round by Enighed. 'Tis Enighed you call it? Round by where like you going Pine Peace.

JB: Ohhh, yes I remember when the dump used to be in Cruz Bay. It was across from where the WAPA generator and the Marketplace are now.

AW: That's right. That's right. Take it to Enighed, I think it was Enighed, well anyhow, take it there to dump, because the water at that time from the pond was almost in the road!

JB: Almost up to where the generator is now?

AW: Yes.

AW: Yes. So then we start putting garbage there as they start to fill in the pond.

JB: Ohhhh.

AW: Is true. And Mr. Jacob was the one who used to do the cleaning. I used to drive the truck. At that time it was under the Sanitation Department. They took care of all the things. They used to send a man up once a week to go round make inspection of cisterns and tanks and everything within the area for sanitary purposes. Then, uh, as I said before it was under the

Sanitation. So after a while, I think it was Mr. Julius Sprauve was the one who recommend that I should get a little compensation for doing that. Because I went to St. John purposely for operating and maintaining two generators that they had there for electrical purposes.

JB: Two generators?

AW: Yes. It was. One alternated, you know. For alternation. And then he decided I should get some compensation for that because I does the two things. And then he made the necessary recommendation and I started to get a little money from the Sanitation Department for doing that.

THE FIRE BRIGADE

AW: Then after that I got in touch with Mr. Boreham and I asked him 'bout a pump, tank that I had seen down in Public Works in St. Thomas, 'cause, before I went to St. John, I worked to Public Works. And he say, "O.K. You want it up there, so O.K." He say, "I'll clean it up and have it ready and I'll ship it up." Told him what I wanted to do, he say "Fine." So then when it came to St. John I had it filled with water and then I got some of my friends: Robert O'Connor, Herman Sprauve, Tony Boynes to act as firemen and we tried to introduce a fire brigade.

I would hook this 50-60 gallon tank on to the dump truck and sometimes go round the city practicing to take care of a home, small house fire, or things like that. Take it on the wharf and make various switches and pump water out of the sea through the hoses and what not.

JB: You had pumped sea water

AW: through the line, not in the tank, just practicing, you know? And, 'cause I knew how to handle that. I was a fireman in St. Thomas before I went to St. John to work. At that time when you go to work to Public Works, it was Public Works and Fire Department. All who worked in the Public Works yard where the machines and thing were was assigned Public Works and Fire Department. We all had assignment when there was a fire. I used to drive a water truck. So I was aware of all those things.

GAME WARDEN

Then after establishing the brigade, Mr. Simmonds, who used to be harbor master at that time, came to St. John. And I was recommended by Mr. Sebastian, Rudolph Sebastian, to be game warden in St. John because he knew me from St. Thomas and since I was there we had an incident with the deer in St. John at the time. When they came up to rectify that, after that they recommend me as being the game warden. The incident with the deer were: it was claimed that this deer damaged or killed a jackass over at Julius Sprauve place.

JB: Sieben

AW: Sieben Mandal. So I told them "It's impossible." The man say "How it's impossible, how it could be impossible." I say, "Because a deer don't go near a jackass." And I say, "A jackass ain't gon stand up for a deer to butt him." I say, "A jackass will kick a deer brains out." I say "If it's a female worse. 'Cause if a buck looking to rut with a jackass she gon kill him. That's completely out. That isn't her species at all." At the same time, while we discussing the deer, the deer was right across the road standing up. And they didn't see the deer. Right across from where we were by Julius Sprauve house across the hill the deer was standing right up. I seen the deer. I say, "you all talking 'bout deer, deer, I say you don't know whether you see a deer or not." That time Sergeant Alexander Brown, the officer in charge up there, he say, "You see a deer?" I say, "Yes, see a deer there! See the buck there!" So when he took his gun, I say "Not that!" and I clapped my hands. I say "You don't have no authority to shoot him!" Mr. Sebastian say, "You right. You don't have no authority to shoot him. If he was destructful to anything, a game warden would be appointed to shoot him, not you." So, next week they came back up

Deer

Photo: Oriel Smith

and they gave me my badge that I was appointed and everything to be Game Warden of St. John.

GUN REGISTRATION

AW: Then I got all who had guns in St. John to bring them in and have them registered. I started it first in St. John. All who had guns. Shotguns. It had lots of shotguns in Cruz Bay. Rellis asked me one time. 'He say "Wha you trying to do?" I say, "No, it's the law." He say, "Well, if it's the law that's something new." I say, "Yes." I say, "See, I'm like a police with this." He say, "all right man", so they start bringing in the guns.

JB: And a lot of local people had guns?

AW: Yes. Yes. A lot of people had shotguns because they used to hunt hogs. It wasn't so much for bird shooting or whatnot. At that time Leinster Bay, and all those places had hogs. Up Hammer Farm. Catherineberg and all them places had hogs. So all those estate owners and thing had guns.

VEHICLE REGISTRATION

AW: I also introduced the inspection of vehicles when they started getting vehicles in St. John.

I told Sargeant Jurgen, at the time, he say "O.K. I with you." And the first person we held up and he didn't want to adhere to the procedure was Corey Bishop. When he brought his jeep in for inspection, they say this jeep brakes got to be fixed. He say, "Uhh, that's in St. Thomas, Austin." Cause he knew that when I was living St. Thomas and working Public Works I used to be an inspector down there.

So Sargeant Leander Jurgen tell him, he say," No. If the inspector say it needs to be repaired, you will repair it or it will not run." So he had get on his high horse. Afterward he had it repaired. Now he know I used to repair vehicles, but because I ground him, he brought a fellow from Tropical Motors up there to repair it. The fellow tell him, yes. He had to change the whole thing. All the brakes was bad, bad, bad.

LEONA

Then I used to have my daughter, Leona, sit on my knee. Driving, sitting down here on my knee. And she would steer the tractor up the hill.

JB: How old was she at the time?

AW: 'Bout 7 years. She could drive from the time she was 8, drive a jeep. When I say drive a jeep I mean drive a jeep! Comfortable.

JB: You used to have her with you

AW: all the time. All the time. Under truck, repairing truck. Everything. She had never played with a doll. She get a doll Christmas morning, through the afternoon time it's take apart, she want to see what's in it. Everything else, my guns, and everything.

I love St. John. If I was a single person, I would have lived in St. John. I might have still been there. But we wanted Leona to go to school and shortly after she was here, in St. Thomas, she went to school—the girls school. Later on she got a very good job in the States. Very, very good job in the States.

THE SIREN

Then after that the siren used to blow in the morning 7 o'clock and then again at 12 o'clock. So after awhile I asked the Sergeant, I say, "Why you don't blow Old Year's Night? That's one night out of the whole year. Blow the old year off. Bring in the new one." He say, "Well, we got to think of it." That year I went up on the ballground with my shotgun and I fired off the year. After that, the second year I did the same thing and then the third year they start to blow the siren. Then it blow every year after that. I don't know if they does it now.

JB: I'm not sure. I don't live in Cruz Bay, so I don't know. But it was a nice custom.

AW: But why? But why? It was a tradition. Here (in St. Thomas) they does blow it.

JB: Maybe they still do it in Cruz Bay, then.

AW: Here they does do it because if ships in port the ships blows their horns, the sirens blow and the church bells ring and everything. It's a mournful situation. While we know what we have passed, we don't know what we are gonna meet, you know.

SHOPPING

JB: Well, how did people live in St. John long ago when there weren't a lot of government jobs, and no hotels?

AW: In those days you could buy a pound of sugar for 5 cents, two pounds of flour for 7 cents. Today what you paying for a pound of flour, shucks you could almost buy a whole bag full. Today they selling banana by the pound. In those days they sell by the bunch.

JB: It's 90 cents a pound now. In some places.

AW: And that used to be for a whole bunch and when I tell you a bunch, a whole big bunch. When I was living in Cruz Bay, Mr. Oswald, Mr. Charles Smith, Mr. Jurgens, Sprauve, any one of them, they knew that I loved flat fish. And I could have received as much as 3 or 4 flat fish any given time from them. Free! They know I always like fried fish. "Wally. Take this, Wally." Because there was nothing, if they want me do something for them, bram! I gone. They can't find a goat, they can't catch a goat, I take my gun, bram! I could shoot the goat for them. Any day. People used to bring pans of pigeon peas, okra, potato, whatever they had, bring me down and I go help them whatever they want to do. Yeah. I decided I was one of them and I helped them as much as I could. That's right.

JB: So tell me, in those days, you were talking about people giving you fish and peas and different things like that, we still don't really have a supermarket like the kind that you have in St. Thomas, Pueblo and Grand

Union. But we have some mini-markets, mini-super-markets and so forth. But how was it when you were up there when your wife had to go to the store to shop. How many grocery stores were there in Cruz Bay? ....

AW: Just two. Charles Smith's and Julius Sprauve's. But Sprauve shop scarcely used to have anything in the groceries because he scarcely used to be there.

JB: He was a Senator at the time?

AW: Yes! Yes! Is only when he come from St. Thomas in the afternoon he stay there, he open it a little, some of the boys dem know he open it they go, they sit and chat with him, have a couple of beers, things like that. And the next morning I take him to Coral Bay. He had a store in Coral Bay.

BOBBY BASTIAN'S FUNERAL

AW: Bobby Bastian was a very nice friend of mine too. Lindbergh father, you know Lindbergh?

JB: Yes. I don't remember Mr. Bastian as much as Miss Dorcas, his wife. I remember her.

AW: Oh, boy, there was nothing they had that I couldn't get. Nothing! Nothing! Bobby Bastian—and he had like to wrassle with me. And do you know the day that I buried him, I had the dikunce to lift up his coffin?

JB: Was he a big man?

AW: Yes! Yes, about my size. And that day to bury him, cause he insist that I bury him, and that day when I lift the coffin, I had hell to get it up! Or get it up and walk with it, I said, "Oh my God I can't carry this no more. I need help." Deenie said, "Hit it!"

JB: Hit it?

AW: Hit the coffin. I say, "Man." She say "HIT IT!" And I hit it. And I came to the graveyard as if I didn't have nothing in my hand.

JB: Well

AW: Hit the box!

JB: Well, what did hitting it

AW: I don't know. Don't ask me. Don't ask me.

JB: But she knew why she told you to do it?

AW: Yeah. She know we used to as people in those days would say "skylark."

JB: Ohhhh. So instead, you didn't have him to hit, so you had to hit

AW: hit the box.

JB: Yeah, O.K.

AW: Hit the box and it came as light as light, "What happen, Stino?" I say, "All right now Man, Ah dunno what it is?" I came straight to the grave. Cause we walked from the church to the graveyard with it.

JB: By the Lutheran Church?

AW: That's right. Right there in Cruz Bay. Eddie Moorhead, Tony Boynes, who it was? somebody else. Neptune Richards. Walked comfortable with him. Certain nights, like Saturday night or so, the same gang, Victor Sewer, we used to go down to his place, the cafe, he tell Dorcas, Well uhh, she say, "Ah know, ah know, ah know." Remain there, knock off 12 o'clock. Or sometimes I leave the generator working and I go down there, we sit down we have a good time. Yeah. Yeah.

RAISING GOATS

AW: I had a good life in St. John. And as I said before, if I didn't have a family, I might have still been in St. John. Because I didn't have NO headache in St. John. None whatsoever. I go where I want, eat what I want. Louis Encarnacion, he got a daughter named Rosa married to um Miss Mildred son.

JB: Mm hm. Irvin.

AW: Irvin. He and I, I don't think brothers would be any closer than he and I were. Very, very close. At one

Goat

time, I believe we had the most goat in Cruz Bay.

JB: Mr. Louis had goats?

AW: Mine. Mine and his.

JB: You used to keep them

AW: over by his place. One time, uh I told him. I say" Louis, whatever you want to do with the goats, do. Sell. Eat." I say, "But save some for me." He say, "Yeah man." But then they wanted me to come over there and draw water for the goat dem every morning and feed the goat dem, go cut bush and thing for the goat dem and everything. I say, "Then for your portion of the goat dem what you gon do?" I say, "I thought I gave you these goat for half increase. Since you have the land, you got wild tamon bush, grass and thing like that you could rear the goat dem here you could develop good good goat here, you could sell when you want to sell and everything. You have all the privilege."

JB: Mm hm

AW: I say and it's just half increase.

JB: Yeah.

AW: The lady say "Man, well I don' know." I say, "O.K. No quarrel, no fight. The butcher came up the Saturday. The goat dem were still in the pen. A lot of goat. I say, "All the old mothers and old rams—kill them." I say, "All dem kid, half of dem is his." "But what you gon do wid the kid dem?" I say he could keep all the kids. Kid what done nurse and thing like that? Let him keep all of them. The older ones go. He say, "Man what you doing. You selling them?" I say, "Yes." I say, "I can't come come draw water for them."

JB: Yeah.

AW: I say, "You mean to say that you can't do it before you go to work? I must come to do it? When you come in the afternoon from work you can't …"

THE DONKEY

AW: I had a donkey. Fellow wanted me to come up

Adrian to check on the donkey. I say, "And you using it every night to go Coral Bay?" I say, "O.K." Went up with the truck, went with the donkey, take off the rope he had on it, put on my rope...I lance her the rope. Down the hill, donkey behind the truck

JB: Ha, ha, ha.

AW: Sell it.

JB: Yeah.

AW: I don't quarrel with people.

JB: They say action speaks louder than words.

Mr. Walters was born in St. Thomas to Edward Walters and Rosalia Peterson. After graduating from Sts. Peter and Paul school in eighth grade, he studied carpentry, plumbing, blueprint-making and building construction.

He worked at the Paiewonsky Bay Rum Distillery in an effort to support his mother and brothers, Richard and Juanito Walters. Other places of employment by the age of 17 were the Civilian Conservation Corps (CCC) Camp as assistant carpenter and machinery operator.

Austin met Ione George in 1942, fell in love and got married. He enlisted in the U.S. Army, becoming a sharp-shooter and returned home after World War II ended. He then worked as a machinist and electrical welder in the Public Works Department.

When St. John received two diesel generating plants to provide electrical power for Cruz Bay, Mr. Walters was tapped to be the operator of the units. He moved with his wife and daughter to St. John.

He was a true pioneer: island explorer and civil servant who looked at government departments in Cruz Bay and enabled new services that St. Thomians took for granted.

His immediate family includes daughter, Leona Walters-Charles; son, Keith; grandchildren, Denise and Harold and great-granddaughter, Shyanne.

Appendix
Excerpts from the *Virgin Islands Daily News*

MORE ATTENTION TO ST. JOHN

Acting Governor Robert Lovett, Chief Municipal Physician Dr. Knud Knud-Hansen and Superintendent of Public Works Donald Boreham spent the entire day in St. John yesterday making an investigation on the need of a clinic building at Coral Bay and Cruz Bay. The need for a new hospital at Cruz Bay was noted by the officials, also a clinic building at Coral Bay.

Projects have been set up in the past for these improvements, and they will be renewed, with the hope of satisfying the needs of the people of St. John in respect to health and sanitation during the fiscal year.

– The Daily News, April 19, 1940, p. 1

Sixteenth Decennial Census – Preliminary Announcement

POPULATION OF ST. JOHN DECREASING

The population of Saint John Island as of April 1, 1940, according to a preliminary count of the returns for the Sixteenth Census, was 722, as compared with 765 on April 1, 1930.

The number of farms (including truck, dairy, and poultry farms) reported for this area for 1940 was 30. (A "farm," as the term is used for census purposes, either must be at least three acres in size or must have produced crops and or animal products to the value of at least $100 in 1939.)

The above figures are released by authority of the Director of the Census. Those relating to 1940 are subject to revision after the final check of the returns.

– The Daily News, April 30, 1940, p. 1

Saint John Maladministered
SPECIAL CORRESPONDENT

From time to time many complimentary as well as equally disparaging remarks have been made about the

Virgin Islands. Most of these compliments or attacks were directed at Charlotte Amalie or Saint Croix, but the island of St. John escaped attention, possibly because of its apparent insignificance and unimportance to the economic life of its sister islands, or, perhaps for the fact that politically they stand at zero.

... 1. The roads in the island of St. John are nothing short of donkey trails and others of wider breadth are difficult to travel on due to loose rocks and jutting stumps much too dangerous to limb and life....

2. An inexpensive telephone system should be installed immediately at Cruz Bay. Four or five public telephones should be placed at central points of the island to be used only for emergency purposes, particularly when medical assistance is urgently needed....

The present radio telephone now in operation for official use at the Administrator's home should be reconditioned immediately (See item 4.) The receiving phone now located in the Governor's office, should be removed and installed in the telephone building where an operator will be available both day and night.... the fact that seven hundred lives depend on this unit, the response of the government should be immediate....

4. The argument advanced for years that the Administrator should be a medical man is fallacious. Reputable and proficient medical men, despite the depression, are loathe to bury their talent and stifle their mental progression in a community where 97 percent of its people are strong, healthy, and free of communicable diseases. These professional men who have dedicated their lives to relieve suffering humanity will find no stimulus or satisfaction in viewing tropical scenery or sipping Government House Rum, cocktails and cocoanut water on the spacious porch of the Administrator's retreat which he calls HOME....

The medical supervision of the island of St. John should be controlled by the Commissioner of Health in St. Thomas. Doctors alternating on Mondays, Wednesdays and Fridays should visit this island at a minimum cost of three dollars a day, and still be of greater help to those who are in need of such assistance. In order to get the most out of these visits, it would be necessary (a) to maintain a motor launch at Cruz Bay; this launch to work in unison with the public telephones and radio-telephone; (b) if a doctor is needed in an emergency, the motor launch will be dispatched at once to Red Hook as the call on the radio-phone is being put through to St. Thomas. If the patient should be at a distant point, the launch will take the doctor to the nearest approach, and from there a waiting horse and messenger will take him to the bedside....

5. The attention of the Governor of the Virgin Islands is called to the fact that if ever a community deserved the boon of electrification, the island of St. John should be placed at the head of the list. It can not be disputed that the gratitude of these poor unfortunates would follow the Chief Executive if he would use his official influence and urge the officials of the Rural Electrification Association to consider St. John's dire necessity of this priceless gift to man — light.

– *The Daily News*, September 4, 1940, pp. 2, 7

Administration Comments on Problems Facing St. John

There has been comment lately in the Press in regard to the administration of the island of St. John. It will be recognized that the administration of the Islands from a governmental, medical, or educational point, is difficult because of the widely scattered settlements which need to be served, and the deplorable facilities for movement throughout the islands, where there are literally no practicable roads.

In a letter to the Honorable Rene L. DeRouen, Chairman of the Committee on the Public Lands, House of Representatives, the Honorable E.K. Burlew, Acting Secretary of the Interior, writes.

"This Island, one of the Virgin Islands group, is ideally suited for national recreational area purposes because of its rugged beauty, and probably no finer beaches exist anywhere in the world. Bathing, boating, fishing, biking, and horseback riding are important forms of recreation offered in this area. The island has an excellent trail system, there being no motorized travel, and it is easily accessible by boat from all directions."

– *The Daily News,* September 9, 1940, p. 7

New Rates For Light, Power Effective Friday

Effective Friday, November 1, 1940, rates for electric light and power in the Municipality as fixed by the Public Utilities Commission, will be eleven cents for light, including street lighting and six cents per KWH for power.

There is no charge for the use or rental of meters and a minimum charge of 50¢ a month for consumption up to four & a half KWH have been made by the Commission.

Special power rates for consumers using double-tariff meters and consuming more than 100 KWH monthly have been set.

– *The Daily News,* October 30, 1940, p. 1

PUBLIC WORKS DEPARTMENT

f. Leopold Jacobs, as Handyman, at a salary of $270.00 per annum, effective November 16, 1940.

– *The Daily News,* November 25, 1940, p. 10

St. John: The Neglected Island

It is true that the revenue from St. John is very small. However, is the revenue from St. Thomas so very much larger as to warrant the great difference in various expenditures on these two islands? Are road building and other improvements financed from local revenue? No! Where does most, of the money for such purposes come from? Is it not Washington?

Isn't it intended that St. John shall share in the funds appropriated by Washington for the Virgin Islands? It doesn't appear so.

How much attention is being paid to St. John by the Municipal Council? Very little. After all, the Municipal Council is composed of seven men, six of whom are from St. Thomas. Are these men as a body interested in their sister island? Apparently not.

The people of St. Thomas are still occasionally complaining about their streets and roads. I suggest that they take a good look at the roads in St. John before crying, about road conditions here. Last June 1 went to St. John, riding from Caneel Bay to Mary's Point. On the way I suffered the loss of a pair of glasses. On the Maho Bay to my home a tree had fallen across the road. In attempting to pass around this tree, a branch brushed off my glasses. They fell to the road and broke into many pieces. Where would such an accident would happen on St. Thomas roads? Nowhere.

The Municipal Council has recently appropriated money for the renovation of the Lange Building, for the erection of a refrigeration plant on the site of the former Hotel Italia, for a wall around Emancipation Garden. All this for St. Thomas. What for St. John?

Even walking is dangerous on some of the roads of St. John. There is danger from low overhanging limbs. There are trees from 6 ft. to 9 ft. high in the middle of the road. When one asks the Administrator to do something about the roads of St. John, he answers with much sympathy, "What more can I do? I have asked over and over any number of times for money to clear the roads. If they don't give us any, what more can I do?"

The new Municipal Council is composed of business men on whose sound judgment the people of St. John count a great deal. They help put them in office because they believe that these men will give them square deal. It is greatly to be hoped that a little more attention will be paid to the neglected little island of St. John by a fair and interested Council.

A ST. JOHNIAN
– *The Daily News,* December 9, 1940, p. 7

Incident Illustrates Urgent Need For Easy Communication With St. John

Asked today his reactions concerning his experience in the breakdown of the motor boat at St. John, Roy Bornn, Superintendent of Social Welfare, said that the incident was without any immediate danger to the party but that it emphasized for him the serious and distressing isolation of the people in St. John, without dependable quick communication either within St. John or between St. John and St. Thomas. From Coral Bay, it is more difficult to communicate with St. Thomas than it is to do so from New York! Safe at Emmaus where the boat's motor failed to start for the return journey, the principal concern was that relatives in St. Thomas, having no means even of uncertaining their whereabouts, must worry about their safety. The fastest means to get word to Cruz Bay was by horse, and from that point by radio communication. Translate this situation into an emergency arising in St. John involving life or limb, and one realizes the distressing handicaps that make life hard for the people of that island. Surely, this Municipality must make a determined effort to provide soon:

(a) A road suitable for vehicular (traffic connecting at least Cruz Bay and Coral Bay.

(b) Radio communication between St. Thomas and at least Cruz Bay, St. John, available at all times, plus either telephone or radio telephone communication between at least Coral Bay and Cruz Bay available at all times.

(c) A dependable boat service between the Islands. Fortunately, the break-down occurred at the dock.

Imagine the increased risks of such engine failure if it had occurred rounding Ram's Head!

— *The Daily News*, January 29, 1947, pp. 1, 4

Cruz Bay to Have Electric Light in Feb.

Cruz Bay will be lighted with electricity for the first time during the month of February, the Acting Governor announced today. Two AC plants which were ordered a year ago have been received and will be installed by the St. Thomas Electric Company here who has the contract to also set up the distribution system in the town. One of the two 20 KW plants were originally scheduled to be installed in Coral Bay but the decision of Caneel Bay Plantation to purchase current from Cruz Bay plant made it necessary for the municipality to use both plants in Cruz Bay. A small unit for Coral Bay has been ordered.

— *The Daily News,* January 31, 1947, p. 1

St. John Gets Electric Light Thursday

The light plant in Cruz Bay will be officially put into service on Thursday next week. An appropriate program marking the first time that the island will be served with electric energy is being planned. The light plant will be in operation for a few hours every night after that date until arrangements have been completed to hook up private users.

— *The Daily News,* April 29, 1947, p. 1

ST. JOHN MOVES FROM DARKNESS TO LIGHT:
Governor, Councilman Throw Switches

While the band played triumphant music Governor Hastie and Councilman Julius Sprauve threw the switches which in the words of energetic Administrator George Simmons brought St. John "out of darkness into light". The occasion was a significant one for the once neglected island and was marked by an interesting program which also was devoted to the dedication of a bandstand located on the newly made playground. Led by the Community Band, the Governor and members of the legislature, the gathering filed into an impromptu parade and marched through the principal streets of the town, returning to the bandstand where the program was concluded.

In thanking one and all for the joint effort in making it possible for St. John to have its own modern light plant, Administrator George Simmons declared that now the people could move about knowing that they do so with the full assurance that each step is accompanied with confidence.

Speakers on the program were Governor Hastie, Bandmaster Alton A. Adams, Ralph Paiewonsky and Julius Sprauve. Roy P. Gordon was Master of Ceremonies.

– The Daily News, May 2, 1947, pp. 1–2

"On the island of St John a bandstand was built for public recreation exercises. A Diesel electric lighting plant, 110-volts alternating current, with a total capacity of 40 kilowatts, was installed in Cruz Bay for street lights, government agencies, and for furnishing light and power to residents in the small town. In the Coral Bay District of St. John a small generating plant was installed to operate a radio telephone station there."

– Annual Report of the Governor of the Virgin Islands to the Secretary of the Interior: Fiscal Year Ended June 30, 1947, p. 9

Glossary

Banacleva	Curdled milk, somewhat like yogurt.
Bata Bata	A green leafy vine that can be fed to rabbits, pigs, etc.
CCC	Civilian Conservation Corps. A Federal work relief program during the Great Depression that put thousands of Americans to work.
Chalk line	To walk a chalk line means to behave, be obedient.
Coal Pit	Pieces of wood covered with leaves and dirt shaped like a rectangle or cone and burned to make charcoal.
Conch	A type of large snail that lives in a big shell in the sea.
Confirmation	A religious ceremony during which a young person is admitted to full membership in a church.
Coop	To hide and watch someone in a way that they don't see you.
Cooperative	A store in St. Thomas where native handicrafts were bought and sold.
Cow Pen	An area on the North Side in Leinster Bay where a part of Browns Bay, Number Two, Number Ten and the alley to Leinster Bay Beach all met.
Deyn	Colloquial expression that is short for "dey ain't" or "they are not" or "they do not."
Dikunce	Used where you would say "devil" in a general way, like: Where the dikunce did I put my keys?
Down Box	Wooden boxes attached by wire handles to a donkey's saddle. They were used to transport produce, children, etc.
Frigidaire	Refrigerator.
Genip	A small fruit with a soft green shell. Inside is a large seed covered with a clear jelly that may be sweet.
Glus	Craving too much of something, ravenous, greedy.
Ground	A vegetable and fruit garden.

Guava   A round fruit, more or less the size of a lemon, with a lot of small seeds in the pinkish pulp. It is green when young, yellow when ripe.

Guavaberries   A somewhat tart berry, about the size of blueberries, containing one or two seeds and a watery pulp—good for tarts and liquer. In St. John they are black or yellow.

Kallaloo   Thick soup made of green leaves, like spinach, papa lolo or massambay, and okra. Other ingredients long ago were dumplings, salt beef, salt pork, and fried goutou fish. Later pigtail replaced the salt beef and salt pork. Conch and/or shrimp may also be added. It is usually served with fungi, a cornmeal dish akin to polenta. (Papa lolo and massambay may still exist, but would be extremely difficult to locate.) Nowadays it is possible to have seafood kallaloo or pork (pigtail) kallaloo.

Kennep   See genip.

Kerosene Tin   A metal container that may have been used to hold kero-sene oil, but which could be repurposed to boil clothes, carry water in down boxes, measure produce, etc.

Mall   Whitish dirt used for paving roads in St. John before asphalt or concrete were available. Sometimes referred to as white mall.

Maran   A green bush whose leaves are used to wash dishes and whose sap has medicinal properties.

Mesple   A round brown fruit with small, flat black seeds whose size and skin texture is similar to a Kiwi, but is sweeter.

Miland   Area on the North Shore south of Maho Bay.

Mortar and Pestle   A political party in St. Thomas/St. John prior to the establishment of the Democratic Party.

Number Two-Ten   Pasture in Leinster Bay Estate.

Pone	A baked pudding containing grated sweet potato and grated pumpkin.
Quelbe	An indigenous form of folk music that originated in the Virgin Islands, also known as scratch band music or Quadrille that has spread throughout the Caribbean and the U.S.
Saltfish	Salted and dried cod fish, ling fish, etc.
Sankey	A book of religious songs.
Sieben	Pronounced Seeven, old estate at right turn of Esperance Road and 100 yards north-northeast of Fish Bay, in Reef Bay Quarter, St. John.
Skylark	To fool around.
Tam	Beret
Tannia Bush	Leaves of the tannia, a root vegetable. May be used as a green leafy vegetable by itself or in Kallaloo.
Tart	A pie with a sweet crust, whose filling can be any of a number of fruit preserves—guava, pineapple, coco-nut, mango, cashew, etc.
Three Stones	Primitive way of cooking using three large stones in the shape of a triangle with pieces of wood in the cen-ter. The pot sits on the stones.
Two-cent Baby	A small handmade cloth doll.
Whelks	A type of sea snail related to the conch, but smaller.
Wist Reed	Local handicrafts made from the wist vine.
Wingay	Strange, odd, peculiar.

Made in the USA
Monee, IL
15 January 2022

88967668R10086